T0383218

The Economic Theory of Professional Team Sports

The Economic Theory of Professional Team Sports

An Analytical Treatment – Second Edition

Stefan Késenne

Emeritus Professor of Economics, University of Antwerp and Catholic University of Leuven, Belgium

Edward Elgar
Cheltenham, UK • Northampton, MA, USA

Published by
Edward Elgar Publishing Limited
The Lypiatts
15 Lansdown Road
Cheltenham
Glos GL50 2JA
UK

Edward Elgar Publishing, Inc.
William Pratt House
9 Dewey Court
Northampton
Massachusetts 01060
USA

A catalogue record for this book
is available from the British Library

Library of Congress Control Number: 2013958018

ISBN 978 1 78195 538 3   (cased)
ISBN 978 1 78347 529 2   (paperback)
ISBN 978 1 78195 539 0   (eBook)

Typeset by Servis Filmsetting Ltd, Stockport, Cheshire
Printed and bound in Great Britain by T.J. International Ltd, Padstow

Contents in brief

Contents in full

Figures

Tables

Symbols

A	attendance
AC	average cost
AR	average revenue
C	total cost
c	unit cost of talent
c^0	fixed capital cost
cap	salary cap
d	demand
$dist$	distance
E	equilibrium
e	effort
ε	elasticity
g_w	expected number of wins
k, κ	proportionality factors
L	total number of players in a team
l	number of players
λ	advertisers' payment per TV viewer
m	market size
MC	marginal cost
MR	marginal revenue
μ	share parameter
n	number of clubs in a league
NAR	net average revenue
p	price
π	profit
q	quality *or* quantity
R	revenue
RME	rate of monopsonistic exploitation
s	supply
σ	ratio of market sizes or win bonus
t	talent
TV	television
u	utility
U	utility
uo	uncertainty of outcome

v	media revenue or fund
w	season winning percentage
W	welfare
x	large-market team
y	small-market team

Preface to the second edition

In the second edition, the basic structure and analytical approach of the first edition have largely been preserved. Major adjustments are made in Chapter 2 on the product market, where a few new topics are added, such as the optimal league size, and the optimal selling and distribution of broadcast rights. Chapter 3 on the player labour market is almost completely rewritten. Not only is the functional specification of the club revenue function adjusted in order to make it well adapted for the sports industry, but the analysis deals only with the two-team model of the player labour market. The n-team model is moved to an appendix. The two-team approach not only allows a direct graphical presentation of the results, but also makes the textbook more suitable for an introductory course. Throughout the second edition, the more advanced and mathematically burdensome sections are indicated with a (*), or are moved to an appendix and can be skipped in an introductory class.

The other chapters are only slightly adjusted, but, as in Chapter 3, in Chapter 5 all n-team approaches are moved to an appendix.

Hopefully, all errors and mistakes in the first edition have been corrected. I thank some bright students in my sports economics class who made excellent comments to correct and improve the text.

Finally, I apologise to the many colleagues in the field of sports economics who have published important analytical contributions to the theory of professional team sports who are not mentioned in this introductory analytical textbook.

Preface to the first edition

The main objective of this book is to put at my students' disposal a text with a more rigorous and analytical treatment of the theory of professional team sports than is presently on offer. My class on sports economics at the University of Antwerp is taught to undergraduate students in applied economics.

The book concentrates on professional team sports only. It is not a textbook on sports economics, nor a textbook on the economics of team sports, because it does not deal with recreational team sports. The distinction between the professional and recreational sports industry is important because, from an economic point of view, they constitute two different worlds. In professional team sports, the consumer is the spectator who is willing to pay for watching the players playing their games at a stadium or on television. The producer is the club or the league, and the production output is the game or the league championship. The main factor of production is the player, playing is work, and the player is paid for his or her performances. In recreational team sports, the consumer is the player or the sports participant who is willing to pay for his club membership. Playing is consumption. The production output is the service offered by the sports club to the sports participant. In professional team sports, watching sport is the focus of interest, whereas in recreational sports it is practising sport. It goes without saying that an economic analysis of both sports sectors will be fundamentally different.

It is not the ambition of this textbook to be complete, even within the relatively small field of the economic theory of professional team sports. Given that the emphasis is on theory and analysis, little attention is paid to institutions and structural differences between the sports industries in North America, Europe and Australia. Many institutional differences do not touch the basic relationships if the theory is kept on a highly abstract level. Only to the extent that the sports structures do affect the basic hypotheses and dominant relationships of the model will they be addressed.

Apart from the most basic and robust empirical results, which are helpful in specifying the models, empirical applications and verifications of the theory are also left out.

Moreover, in order to stay within the planned volume of this book, many important and interesting topics in sports economics are not covered, because a selection had to be made. Also, in some areas, the literature did not offer a clear theoretical and analytical framework, while in others the mathematical level was too advanced for undergraduate students. To make the theoretical analysis more accessible, simplifying the specification of some relationships was necessary.

Nevertheless, I hope that this textbook fills a gap in the growing market of books on sports economics by providing an analytical approach to the theory of professional team sports. I wish to thank all my colleagues, in particular the many sports economists from Europe and North America who have become good friends. The many discussions I have had with them during international conferences and meetings have been a great help in writing this book.

Finally, for the sake of readability, this book is framed throughout in the masculine gender. This is in no way intended to exclude or denigrate the role of female sports participants.

1

The peculiar economics of professional team sports

1.1   Introduction

The economics of professional team sports is a young and relatively small field of academic research. Simon Rottenberg, an economist at the University of Massachusetts at Amherst, is generally considered to be the pioneer of sports economics with his seminal article on the baseball player market, published in the *Journal of Political Economy* in 1956. After 50 years, and notwithstanding a rapid growth in the number of sports papers over the last few decades, Rottenberg's article still looks remarkably up to date, and is a must on every reading list for students of sports economics. Another pioneer in the short history of economic thought on team sports is Walter Neale with his paper 'The Peculiar Economics of Professional Sports', published in the *Quarterly Journal of Economics* in 1964. Surprisingly enough, both economists did not publish any other significant contribution to the field. In the late 1960s and early 1970s, other economists took over and continued to publish regularly on the subject: James Quirk, Gerald Scully and Roger Noll in the USA; Colin Jones in Canada; Peter Sloane in the UK; and Braham Dabscheck in Australia. A milestone in economic research on professional team sports was a book edited by Roger Noll (1974c), *Government and the Sports Business*. This collection of excellent papers, presented at probably the first conference ever on sports economics, has inspired a growing number of economists, including myself, to concentrate on team sports. To the best of my knowledge, 'Pay and Performance in Major League Baseball', written by Gerald Scully (1974), was the first monograph on sports economics, although the doctoral dissertation of H.G. Demmert (1973), *The Economics of Professional Team Sports*, is often overlooked as an important early contribution to the theory. Almost 20 years later, two other important monographs were published: *Pay Dirt: The Business of Professional Team Sports*, by James Quirk and Rodney Fort (1992), and *Baseball and Billions*, by Andrew Zimbalist (1992).

At the turn of the century, a new journal, called *The Journal of Sports Economics*, saw the light in California, with Leo Kahane as chief editor. It mainly published studies and papers on professional team sports. Since then, a growing number of sports conferences have been organised, and new books and conference proceedings have been published, so that gradually sports economics has become a fully developed field of research. A two-volume book, *The Economics of Sport*, edited by Andrew Zimbalist (2001), presents an excellent collection of papers written between 1950 and 2000. A follow-up, *Recent Developments in the Economics of Sport*, was edited by Wladimir Andreff (2011).

1.2 Peculiarities

When a new field of research takes off, the first question to be asked is whether there is any justification for devoting a separate field of economic research to professional team sports. Is there anything special or exceptional about the industry? Neale (1964) pointed to the most important economic characteristic that makes the industry of professional team sports different from other industries. He called it the **inverted joint product**. Economists are familiar with 'joint production': one single production process yields two or more different products. 'Inverted joint production' refers to a situation where two production processes by two companies are needed to produce and supply one single product. In team sports, the companies are the sports clubs, and the product is the game. One team cannot play a football match; it needs an opponent team. If the product is not just one individual game but also the league championship, more than two clubs are necessary.

Moreover, sport is basically about competition. If the playing strengths of two teams are too far apart so that one team always wins without much competition, the product is not very interesting for people to watch. So, a second peculiar characteristic of the industry is that a certain degree of competitive balance between the teams is necessary in order to market and sell the product. A sport loses its attractiveness if there isn't any uncertainty of outcome in a championship. Although there is some disagreement among sports economists about the optimal degree of competitive balance (see Szymanski, 2003), it cannot be denied that a minimum of outcome uncertainty is necessary. Watching your home football team win by 12 goals to 0 can be great fun once, but no real sports fan wants to experience the same huge score in each game, week after week.

These two characteristics of the team sports industry have had serious consequences for the competition policy on product and labour markets. If more clubs are involved in supplying the product, such as a league championship, some cooperation between the clubs is necessary. It is obvious that a well-organised championship is more interesting to watch than a number of occasional individual games. So, some regulation of the product market is called for. How many clubs can enter the product market, and under what conditions? How many times is the product to be supplied to the public, and which clubs will meet when and where? Club owners come together and create a union, a federation or a league, which is, in economic terms, a cartel of clubs. If more than one league is created, they merge after a time, so that, in most sport disciplines, a monopoly league becomes the rule. Economists, however, cherish competition and competitive markets, and are opposed to cartels and monopolies because they cause a welfare loss by charging prices that are too high and by limiting production output. Given the existing antitrust legislation, the question is if the team sports industry is entitled to an antitrust exemption. Whereas the business strategy of firms in most sectors of the economy is to get rid of fierce competitors in order to build a strong and comfortable market position, the same strategy in the sports industry would kill the business, because a sports team needs opponents of more or less equal strength.

Competition on the player labour market has also come under fire. Without free entry to the product market and free relocation of teams, it is argued that a free player market threatens the competitive balance in the league because a rich club with a local monopoly position in a large-city market can hire all the best players by offering the highest salaries. So, a free player labour market would destroy the sports business. Moreover, the hiring of playing talent by a team creates negative external effects. Team owners do not always realise and take account of the fact that strengthening their own teams weakens the opponent teams in the league.

Neale (1964) concluded from these considerations that the team sports industry shows some characteristics of a natural monopoly. He also claimed that the league, and not the club, should be the single production entity and the employer of the players, so that the league can allocate the players to the clubs, as the league's local branches, in order to guarantee the necessary uncertainty of outcome. Most sports economists, however, as well as many sports jurists (see Ross, 1991), disagree. Even if they accept that a monopoly league is not necessarily anticompetitive, they do not approve of the creation of local monopoly positions for clubs, the strict limitation of the number of teams in the top league, the restrictions to the freedom of players to move to other teams, the pooling of television rights by the league, and so on (see Noll, 1999). In most professional team sports, the clubs are largely independent entities and the employers of the players, but the sports league tries to control and regulate the product and player market. The most common market regulations are the restrictions on player mobility by creating a so-called reservation system or retain-and-transfer system. There are also different arrangements to share revenues among clubs, and leagues impose salary or payroll caps. These corrections to the free market outcomes aim to improve the attractiveness of the games, by guaranteeing a reasonably competitive balance in the league, and to hold down top players' salaries.

Given the peculiarities of the professional team sports industry, the question can be raised as to whether the common firm objective of profit maximisation in microeconomic textbooks is also what sports teams are aiming at. Is a sports team owner not more interested in winning, and what are the implications?

1.3   Objectives of team owners

In professional team sports, clubs can have different objectives and they lead to different outcomes in terms of distribution of talent among teams, player salary level, total league revenue, ticket price and so on. Also the impact of most market regulations on these variables is different. The most common firm objective in economic theory is profit maximisation. In the United States, most analysts assume that professional sports clubs behave as profit maximisers (Rottenberg, 1956; Noll, 1974c; Quirk and Fort, 1992; Vrooman, 1995). One of the most important decisions club managers have to make is the hiring of talent. More talents increase not only the season cost of a club but also the winning record and the season revenue. So, clubs will hire the number of playing talents that maximises the difference between season revenue and season cost. If π indicates season profits, the objective is:

$$\max \pi = \max(R - C), \qquad (1.1)$$

where R is total season revenue and C is total season cost. Assuming that the number of talents of the team is the only decision variable, the optimality condition for profit maximisation is that the marginal revenue of talent equals the marginal cost. A club maximises its profits if the increase in total revenue by hiring one more talent is equal to the increase in the total cost of one more talent. As long as the marginal revenue is higher than the marginal cost, the club can increase its profit by hiring more talent.

In Europe, sports economists have raised serious doubts about profit maximisation as a realistic objective in professional sports. Although professional sports clubs in the North American major leagues are more businesslike than in the European football leagues, some US economists seem to have their doubts as well (see Quirk and El-Hodiri, 1974; Rascher, 1997; Zimbalist, 2003). Sloane (1971) asserted that European football clubs do not behave as profit maximisers, but rather as utility maximisers. He observed that many owners of European football clubs consider spending money on their team as a consumption activity. As consumers, club owners act as if they are maximising a utility function, where other variables, beside profits, appear as arguments; this might include playing success, stadium attendance, competitive balance, youth development, community building and so on.

Késenne (1996, 2000a), in an attempt to make the utility-maximising model more operational, selected the winning percentage, which he considered to be the most important variable in Sloane's utility function to be maximised by team owners and managers, as the sole objective. Professional football clubs in Europe are most of all interested in winning, and the best way to achieve that goal is to hire the best players, or in other words to maximise the number of playing talents under certain restrictions. One restriction is that a club has to stay within the limits of its budget. As a first approximation, the breakeven condition can be imposed, that is, total revenue equals total cost. However, this condition is not necessary for the application of the win-maximisation model. One can assume that a club has to guarantee a certain profit rate in order to satisfy the owners or the shareholders. A club can be profitable without being a profit maximiser. Also, the win-maximisation model does not exclude season losses because, as a consumer, the owner can be prepared to spend money on the team. In its most simple form, this objective function can be written as:

$$\max w \text{ subject to: } R - C = \pi^0, \tag{1.2}$$

where w is the season winning percentage of the team and π^0 is a fixed amount of positive or negative profits. A fixed amount of profits also implies a fixed profit rate, because the capital stock is considered to be constant in the short run. So, the breakeven condition is only a special case where profits π^0 are zero.

Another variant of the utility-maximisation model has been proposed by Rascher (1997), who assumed that sports clubs are maximising a linear combination of profits and wins, which can be written as:

$$\max (\pi + \alpha w) \text{ with } \alpha > 0. \tag{1.3}$$

Because the weight parameter α can be different for every club, it allows clubs to be more profit orientated (α < 1) or more win orientated (α > 1). This model is comparable with the win-maximisation model, which also includes the possibility of a certain profit rate.

So far, most empirical tests have failed to be conclusive in accepting or rejecting the profit- or the win-maximisation hypothesis, because these tests are based on the pricing rule or the price elasticity (see Noll, 1974c; Ferguson et al., 1991; Alexander, 2001). However, as will be shown in Chapter 4, the pricing rule of a win-maximising team is the same as the pricing rule of a profit-maximising team.

More recently, a different empirical test has been developed by Garcia-del-Barrio and Szymanski (2009), who estimated the best responses of soccer clubs in the Spanish and the English leagues over a period of ten seasons. They found that choices are more closely approximated by win maximisation than by profit maximisation.

Recently, Paul Madden (2012) proposed another interesting club objective, which he called fan welfare maximisation, referring to the existence of members' clubs in European football (*Vereins* in Germany). Subject to a nonnegative profit constraint, these clubs aim to maximise the aggregate utility of their fans. Madden also shows that, under certain hypotheses and in the absence of capacity constraints, fan welfare maximisation is equivalent to maximising match attendance, which is a positive function of talent and a negative function of the ticket price.

One might wonder if these club objectives make such a difference. Is hiring the best players not the best way to increase winning percentage, match attendance, club revenue and profits? And is maximising profits not the best way to raise the money to hire and pay the best players? A simple diagram shows that win and profit maximisation do make a difference in hiring the optimal number of playing talents. Figure 1.1 shows the different talent demand levels emerging from different club objectives. The number of talents is indicated on the horizontal axis and total season revenue and cost on the vertical axis. Obviously, the total cost increases with the number of talents. Also a club's total revenue increases as the club becomes more successful, but the revenue function is assumed to be concave in the number of talents. If a team becomes too strong, public interest fades because of a lack of uncertainty of outcome, and total revenue can decrease.

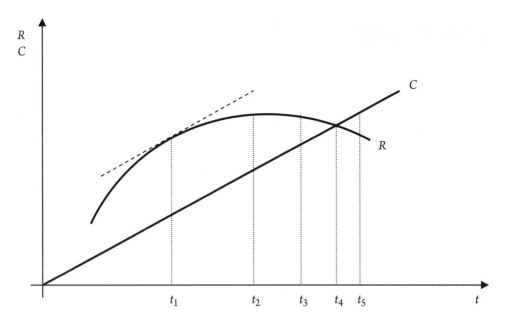

Figure 1.1 Club objectives

A profit-maximising club will hire t_1 playing talents, where marginal revenue, which is the slope of the revenue function, equals marginal cost, which is the slope of the cost function. A revenue maximiser will hire t_2 talents. A win-maximising club under the breakeven constraint will hire t_4 talents, where total cost equals total revenue. If a certain profit rate is necessary, the club can hire t_3 talents. If the owner is prepared to lose money on his team, he can hire t_5 talents.

EXERCISES 1

Assume the following quadratic revenue function and the linear cost function in terms of talents $R = 10t - t^2$ and $C = 2t$.

Derive the optimal number of talents and also the profits of:

1.1 a profit maximiser
1.2 a revenue maximiser
1.3 a win maximiser
1.4 a maximiser of a linear combination of profits and wins with a = 3.

2

Sports product market

2.1 Introduction

The product market in the professional team sports industry is the market of games and league championships. In most countries and professional sports disciplines, a monopoly league seems to be the rule. Whenever rival leagues show up in a country, they tend to merge after a time or cooperate and act as if they are one single league. Most sports economists, even advocates of more competition in sports, seem to accept this fact, and do not consider a monopoly league as necessarily anticompetitive (see Noll, 1999). In North American professional sports, all closed major leagues are monopoly leagues. In Europe, where multiple national leagues coexist, all structured hierarchically by a system of relegation and promotion, the highest division in each country can be considered as a monopoly league. Notwithstanding the European Union and its common market for goods, services and capital, the national product markets of professional team sports are still protected from foreign competition. We will therefore only concentrate on the product market of games in a championship that is organised by a monopoly league. The producers and the suppliers of the sports product are the clubs; the consumers and the demanders of the sports product are the spectators and the fans. The product can be purchased or consumed by attending a game in a stadium or by watching it on television. The stadium visitors pay a ticket price to enter the ball park. Watching a game on television can be free or paid for. Open-air television by state-owned companies is mainly paid by general taxation or a specific television tax. Privately owned broadcasting companies can attract TV advertising, paid by different companies and industries to market their products, but can also charge a price; this can be the viewer's subscription fees or pay-per-view. Television companies can broadcast a full match, live or recorded, or only the highlights.

2.2 The league championship

In almost every country, the product market of professional team sports is strictly regulated by the league, so that it can be considered as a cartel of clubs (see Sloane, 1971). This is often justified by the peculiar economics of the industry. Although most economists accept that a certain degree of cooperation between the clubs in a league is inevitable, they do not agree with all the regulations and restrictions that are imposed by the league, as will be explained later on.

One of the important restrictions is the lack of free entry to the market whatever the profitability of the participating clubs. The number of clubs in the North American major leagues or in the highest national divisions in the European countries is officially fixed, and can only be changed by a formal agreement between the clubs in the league. An interesting issue is the optimal number of teams in a league, and the question is whether this number can be left to the participating clubs to decide. It is obvious that in most cases the insiders want to keep the outsiders at bay, and that the stronger teams want to eliminate some of the weaker teams, certainly if revenues are shared among teams in a league. From the perspective of teams, leagues and society, it is not clear what the welfare implications of league contraction are (see Noll, 2003).

Another restriction is that clubs are not free to choose their location. In most US major leagues and European national leagues, teams are not free to move without formal permission from the league. This has serious consequences, because it gives the clubs in large cities a permanent advantage over the clubs in small towns. It also forces an ambitious team that wants to move up to stay in its small market. An important consequence of this restriction is not only that it can cause a lasting competitive imbalance in a league, but also that most clubs are local monopolists in their region.

Some of these regulations can be countered, to a certain extent, by the European system of relegation and promotion, whereby the teams at the bottom of the final ranking are relegated to a lower division, and the champions of the lower divisions are promoted to a higher division. This way, the local monopoly position of a team in a large market, or a region with a large drawing potential, can be broken. Relegation and promotion also create more incentives for the low-ranked teams to perform, because demotion to a lower division often implies a dramatic budget reduction (see Noll, 2002).

Clubs are also not free to determine their production output and the supply of their product on the market. It is the league that organises the championship and decides when, where and how many times teams have to play. These restrictions do not seem to bother most economists, because they agree that a well-organised championship is far more interesting for fans to watch than a number of random matches.

2.2.1 Uncertainty of outcome and competitive balance

The uncertainty of outcome, or the competitive balance in a league, is one of the most discussed and controversial issues in sports economics. Competition on the playing field is a basic ingredient of sports. In the literature, three levels of uncertainty of outcome have been distinguished: match uncertainty; seasonal uncertainty or within-season uncertainty; and championship uncertainty or between-season uncertainty (see Cairns et al., 1986; Sanderson, 2002; Szymanski, 2003; Kringstad and Gerrard, 2007).

Match uncertainty is often measured by looking at the square of the difference in winning percentages or league standings of the two teams. The idea is that, if the winning percentages of the two teams are too far apart, there is less uncertainty of outcome, which reduces fan interest. Jennett (1984) developed a within-season measure of uncertainty, which he used to explain match attendance. It not only indicates whether both teams are still in the running to win the championship, but also takes into account the number of games left before the closing of the championship.

Seasonal or within-season uncertainty is often approached by a parameter that is linked to the standard deviation (SD) of the winning percentages of the teams in the league. The smaller the SD, the smaller is the spread of winning percentages and the closer the competition. Because the SD, with the same degree of imbalance, increases with the number of games played, the Noll–Scully SD ratio, which corrects for the number of games, is often used. It is given by $\frac{SD}{0.5/\sqrt{m}}$, where m is the number of games played. The denominator measures the 'ideal' (perfect balance) SD. This 'ideal' SD is based on a binomial distribution of the number of games won (see Fort and Quirk, 1995). A problem with the Noll–Scully SD ratio is not only that it cannot be applied if the games allow ties, but also that it can be, in some applications, significantly smaller than one, whereas theoretically its minimum value is one. A more appropriate and elegant measure has been proposed by Kelly Goossens (2006), which is the ratio of the actual SD and the SD in the case of a perfect imbalance or a perfect predictability of outcome. The value of this indicator, which she named NAMSI (National Measure of Seasonal Imbalance), lies between zero and one. The closer to zero, the higher is the seasonal uncertainty. The advantage of this measure is that comparisons can be made between leagues with a different number of teams and games and that it is also applicable in championships allowing ties.

The championship or between-season uncertainty is a dynamic measure which takes into account more than one season. Even if, over a number of consecutive seasons, the standard deviations of the winning percentages are always the same, it can hide totally different situations. It is possible that the same teams always end on top, but also that, in each season, another team ends on top. A simple way to measure this uncertainty is to count the number of different teams that reach the top or the top three positions in the final ranking over a number of seasons.

Humphreys (2002) has proposed one single measure to combine seasonal uncertainty and championship uncertainty, called the competitive balance ratio. The advantage of just one accurate figure to measure the uncertainty of outcome is tarnished by the disadvantage of losing important information on the kind of imbalance.

In a recent doctoral dissertation, Vasileios Manasis (2012) quantifies different measures of competitive balance in professional team sports, taking into account the specifics of European football, where there is competition not only to win the national championship, but also to qualify for the UEFA Champions League and the Europa League, as well as competition not to be relegated to a lower division. Step by step, the author derives his final bidimensional (in-between and between-season) special dynamic concentration (SDC) index which accounts for the three-level European competition.

Extensive empirical research on the demand for tickets has shown that the impact of match uncertainty and seasonal uncertainty on attendance is not very significant and robust. So far, the championship uncertainty, although few empirical tests exist, turns out to have a more significant positive effect on attendance. Apparently, fans don't like to see the same clubs on top year after year (see Forrest and Simmons, 2002; Garcia and Rodriguez, 2002; Borland and Macdonald, 2003; Krautmann and Hadley, 2004). In a novel and interesting theoretical and empirical approach, starting from the reference-dependent preferences of team supporters, Coates et al. (2012) even rejected the so-called uncertainty of output hypothesis (UOH).

In the appendix to this chapter, an attempt is made to derive theoretically the main parameters that affect the optimal competitive balance in a league.

2.2.2 The optimal number of teams in a league

The optimal size of a sports league is an issue that has been a constant concern of league authorities in European football. There are considerable differences in the number of teams in the top national divisions of European football, ranging from 10 to 20. Although the system of promotion and relegation allows top teams to move up to the first division, it is the monopoly league that decides how many teams compete in the top championship. Over the years, reductions and expansions of the league size have occurred in most European countries and North American major leagues.

An interesting question is which league objective or consideration affects the leagues' decision on the numbers of teams. Although one can observe a small positive correlation between the league size and the country's population, it would be short-sighted to impose a league size that is proportional to the size of the population. Applying this rule to Russia and Luxembourg might result in a spectacular league in Russia and a less-than-spectacular league in Luxembourg with only two teams.

Vrooman (1997) and Szymanski (2003) have analysed the decisions of a monopoly league regarding the size of the league, assuming that league revenue is shared among all participating teams, based on Buchanan's (1965) club theory. Noll (2003) has shown that revenue sharing among the teams creates a strong incentive for clubs to reduce the number of teams in a league. Kahn (2007) points out that, in a free-entry market, the number of teams entering the top division would be higher than the social optimum. The social optimum cannot be attained in a free-entry market because individual teams impose quality externalities on other teams and their fans, by lowering the average team quality. Based on his approach, Kahn (2007) concludes that the optimal league size will be between the free market league size and the monopoly league size, but closer to the free market league size if the supply of playing talent is more elastic. With the open European player market, this might well be the case in the national football leagues in Europe.

In this section, we will compare the welfare optimal number of teams in a league with the number decided by the monopoly league, based on simple and aggregated demand models for spectator sport.

The derivation of the demand function for sport starts from the assumption that every citizen who is interested in the sport championship will watch the games if the price of watching the championship's games, in the stadium or on television, is zero. Let m be the size of the national market or a country's total population, and a the percentage of that population interested in the championship, which is an indicator of the popularity of the championship. If the price/quality ratio goes up, fewer people will be interested in watching the games, depending on the price elasticity, indicated by the parameter b as the slope of a linear demand curve. So, the demand function for the league championship can be written as:

$$d = am - b\frac{p}{q} \qquad 0 \leq a \leq 1, \qquad (2.1)$$

where p is the average price and q in an indicator of the championship attractiveness or quality. The elasticity parameter b is assumed to depend on the average income or the welfare level in the country; it is larger for a poor country and smaller for a rich country. Apart from the price, all variables, population, popularity, quality and the welfare level, have a positive effect on demand. If the price is zero, all interested fans (am) will watch the games. If the league fixes the average price in order to maximise total league revenue, with $R = pd = p(am - b\frac{p}{q})$, the first-order condition can be written as:

$$\frac{\partial R}{\partial p} = am - \frac{2b}{q}p = 0.$$

So, the optimal price is $p^* = \frac{amq}{2b}$, and corresponding demand is $d^* = \frac{am}{2}$. Total revenue is then $R^* = \frac{a^2m^2q}{4b}$.

As can be seen, price and total league revenue are positively affected by the size of the population (m), the popularity of the championship (α), the quality of the league (q) and the welfare level of the country (b). However, the demand is only affected by population and popularity, because quality and welfare differences are compensated for by the level of the price. This demand curve and the optimal price are presented in Figure 2.1.

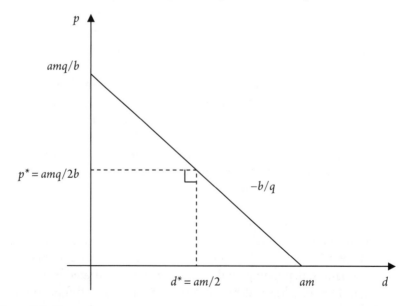

Figure 2.1 Demand curve

The crucial variable of this specification is the quality of the league q. What are the variables that affect league quality q or the attractiveness of the league championship? In the literature, the most important determinants seem to be: 1) the total number of teams in the league and the number of games in the championship; 2) the average talent level of the teams or the average quality of the games; 3) the winning percentages of the teams; and 4) the competitive balance.

The first variable is the number of games. The more games sport-loving spectators can watch, the better it is for the attractiveness of the champion-ship. Also, supporters prefer to watch their favourite team playing in the top league. In the classical European setting where each team plays one home and one away game against all other teams, without play-offs, the number of teams in a league determines the number of games. If the number of teams is n, the total number of games in a season is $n(n-1)$, that is: $2(n-1)$ play days times $n/2$ games per play day.

The average talent level of the teams, and therefore also the average quality of the games, will be higher with a lower number of teams in the league. Given that there is a fixed talent supply (t) in a country during a championship, from both local and foreign origin, the playing talents will be allocated or spread out over a lower number of teams. So, the average quality of the games can be approached by the ratio of total available talent to the number of teams (t/n).

League quality is also positively affected by the winning percentages of the teams. Fans prefer to watch winning teams. With a reduction or an expansion of the number of teams in a league, or by promotion and relegation, it is always a weaker team that has to leave or join the closed major league or the top divi-sion. As a consequence, the winning percentages of the remaining teams are reduced by a contraction of the league size (unless the leaving team is a giant killer). It is a fact that the sum of the winning percentages of all clubs always equals $n/2$.

How is the competitive balance affected by the number of teams? And does the competitive balance affect the quality of the league?

Regarding the first question, the elimination of the weakest teams does affect the competitive balance. In Table 2.1, a numerical example is presented to show this effect. Let's assume that the relative strength of the teams is given by: A>B>C>D>E>F, and that there is a 50 per cent chance that the stronger team beats the next one in the row and a 100 per cent chance that it wins against the weaker teams.

Table 2.1 League contraction: numerical example

League size	Winning percentages						Sum	Range	SD
	A	B	C	D	E	F			
Six teams	0.90	0.80	0.60	0.40	0.20	0.10	3	0.80	0.32
Four teams	0.83	0.67	0.33	0.17			2	0.66	0.30

Starting from a six-team league, the winning percentages can be calculated as presented in the first row of Table 2.1. If the league is reduced to four teams, with the two weakest teams, E and F, leaving or being relegated to a lower division, the adjusted winning percentages are given in the second row.

Both the range and the standard deviation, as simple indicators of the within-season competitive balance, are lower in the contracted league. So, the contracted league is more balanced. However, as observed by Noll (2003), the pennant race in the contracted league is not as close, which makes the competition less balanced. Given these observations, we can assume that the competitive balance is not strongly affected by the number of teams.

Moreover, the empirical research so far has not found very convincing evidence that spectators prefer a more balanced competition (see Borland and Macdonald, 2003; Szymanski and Leach, 2005). Therefore, we leave out the competitive balance as an argument in the quality function.

From the analysis above, and dropping the competitive balance, we can conclude that the quality of the league is mainly affected by the number of games $n(n-1)$, by the average talent level of the teams t/n and by the sum of the winning percentages $n/2$. So, the quality q can be written as a function of n and t. We assume that the number of teams and talent has a positive effect on quality, with a decreasing marginal effect of the number of teams, so:

$$q[n, t] \text{ with } \frac{\partial q}{\partial n} > 0 \quad \frac{\partial^2 q}{\partial n^2} < 0 \quad \frac{\partial q}{\partial t} > 0. \tag{2.2}$$

We can now derive what the number of teams is that will be fixed by the monopoly league in the interest of the participating or insider clubs. Assuming that the marginal cost of a team in the league is constant and equal to c, and that the monopoly league tries to maximise the average net revenue of the teams in the league, or:

$$\max\left(\frac{R - cn}{n}\right) = \max\left(\frac{a^2m^2}{4bn}q[n, t] - c\right),$$

the first-order condition for a maximum is:

$$\frac{\partial q[n, t]}{\partial n} = \frac{q[n, t]}{n}.$$

As indicated by Szymanski (2003), this is equivalent to the solution of the optimal number of workers in a labour-managed firm. The optimal number of teams turns out to be independent of the size of the market, the popularity of the sport and the income level.

In Figure 2.2, where marginal and average quality are drawn as a function of the number of teams, the league's optimal point is found in n_1, where the marginal quality and the average quality curves intersect.

We can also try to derive what the welfare optimal number of teams in a league will be in this model. Based on the demand equation in Figure 2.1, total welfare can be calculated as the sum of league revenue and consumer

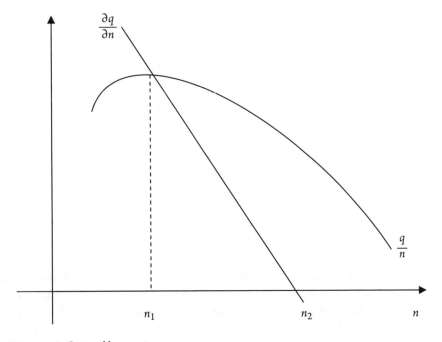

Figure 2.2 Optimal league size

surplus. As can be seen, the consumer surplus (CS) is 50 per cent of total league revenue and equal to $\frac{a^2m^2q[n,t]}{8b}$. So, the welfare level is:

$$W = R + CS = \frac{3a^2m^2q[n,t]}{8b}.$$

Maximising total welfare is then equivalent to maximising quality (q), so the optimum condition is given by:

$$\frac{\partial q[n,t]}{\partial n} = 0.$$

Again, the solution is independent of population, popularity and income, but the available talents in the country do affect the league size. As can be seen in Figure 2.2, the number of teams will now be n_J, which is clearly well above the number of teams fixed by the monopoly league (n_1).

What this simple theoretical model shows is that the number of teams that monopoly league authorities allow to enter the top divisions in European football is well below the number that is optimal for the consumers and the industry from a welfare economic point of view. However, this model has not compared the quality of a championship with 20 teams and 380 games and a championship with only 16 teams and more than 480 games. In some leagues, there are fewer teams and more games. This is an important trade-off that should be considered by league authorities, when deciding about the number of teams. One can opt for a lower number of teams and more games, as in Switzerland and Austria, or for more teams and fewer games, as in two other small countries, Belgium and the Netherlands. With fewer teams there are more high-quality games, which can increase demand, but too many games between the same teams in a championship might also decrease the marginal utility of these games and reduce demand.

Moreover, more teams in the top division will make more spectators happy, because supporters like to see their home-town team play at the top level. Because it is unclear if this negative effect is stronger or weaker than the positive quality effect, we have assumed, for simplicity reasons, that the championship structure is a given fact, which implies that there is a fixed relationship between the number of teams and the number of games, as in the model above. So, even if a championship consists of a high number of games with a limited number of teams, in which case each team plays more matches, the basic conclusion of the model still holds that, with the given structure of the championship, in the presence or absence of play-offs, the number of teams, decided by the monopoly league, will be lower than the welfare-maximising number (see Késenne, 2009b).

Kahn (2007) draws different conclusions: in his model, the expected decrease in average team quality has a strong negative impact in an expanded league, and his model neglects the fact that league expansion can also raise fan demand because it increases the clubs' winning percentages as in Noll (2003). In our model, the impact of expansion on the insider teams' winning percentages is taken into account, but the negative effect of expansion on average team quality might be underestimated, because it is only captured by the decreasing marginal effect of the number of teams on league quality.

If so, the question can be asked whether the decision about the number of teams can be left to a board of league authorities that consists of representatives from only the insider teams. Also, doesn't this monopoly justify some government interference in fixing the number of clubs in the top league? All too often, it is a deliberate policy of the largest and richest teams, which have an important say in the league's management, and do not run any serious risk of being relegated, to limit the number of teams, keeping all the football money as much as possible to themselves and neglecting the interests of supporters and consumers.

2.3 Stadium attendance

In explaining stadium attendance, one can distinguish between at least two different approaches. Besides the study of the season attendance of a club, one can also be interested in explaining the number of tickets sold for each single game. Depending on that choice, other explanatory variables have to be taken into account.

2.3.1 Season attendance

The total season attendance of a club depends first of all on the characteristics of the local market of the club. It is obvious that the drawing potential for spectators of a team in a large city, or a densely populated area, is greater than in a small town. However, it is not only the size of the population that is important; preferences and social stratification can also affect the purchase of stadium tickets. We bring these characteristics together in one variable which we call the size of the market or the drawing potential of the team. We assume that this variable cannot be controlled by club management, so that all considerations regarding a club's marketing policy are left out.

A second variable that is considered very important for club attendance is the performance of the team on the field or its playing success. This variable can be measured by the season winning percentage of the team or the ranking of the team. Fans clearly prefer winning teams over losing teams. However, the winning percentage of a team should not become too high. If a team becomes too strong compared with its opponents, so that the probability of winning approaches unity, there is no longer any uncertainty of outcome in the league championship. Because this can have a negative effect on public interest, the attendance function is assumed to be concave in a team's winning percentage. Winning has a diminishing marginal effect on the demand for tickets. If the winning percentage passes a certain critical value, its effect on attendance can even be negative, so that one can assume that the revenue function is not only concave but also first increasing and then decreasing in winning percentage.

As explained in section 2.2, the uncertainty of outcome (uo) can also be introduced in the demand function model by a more specific variable. One simple indicator is $uo = w(1 - w)$, where w is the season winning percentage of a team. This variable reaches its maximum value ($uo = 0.25$) with maximum uncertainty ($w = 0.5$). It follows that both variables, the winning percentage and the uncertainty of outcome, can be represented in the attendance function by w. Moreover, if the supporters' trade-off between winning percentage and uncertainty of outcome is given by the product of the two variables, utility $u = w^2(1 - w)$, and one can derive that the optimal winning percentage is larger than 0.5, because $\frac{\partial u}{\partial w} = 2w - 3w^2 = 0$, so $w^* = 2/3 = 0.67$ (see also Sandy et al., 2004).

Besides the relative quality of a team, measured by the winning percentage, its absolute playing quality can also affect a club's season attendance. It makes a difference to fans whether their home team is the best one in a high-quality league or the best one in a low-quality league. Spectators like to watch the spectacular performances of the star players even if these stars play for the visiting team. So, the absolute playing quality in the league can be measured by the total sum of talents in the league. In a short-term model, however, this variable can be assumed to be constant, and the same for every team, so it is left out of the model in this section.

The ticket price is also likely to affect the demand for tickets. If sport is a normal good, the lower the ticket price, all else equal, the more tickets will be sold. Obviously, most clubs charge different ticket prices, depending on the position and the comfort of the stadium seat. Clubs also sell season tickets, which reduce the price for attending one game. For simplicity reasons, we take only one ticket price into consideration, which can be considered as the average price to enter the ball park.

So, the attendance function can be specified as:

$$A_i = A_i[m_i, w_i, p_i] \qquad \text{for all } i: 1, n, \qquad (2.3)$$

where A_i is the season stadium attendance of the club i, m_i is the size of its local market, w_i is the season winning percentage of the team, p_i is the average ticket price and n is the number of teams. Based on the discussion above, the following conditions hold for this demand function:

$$\frac{\partial A_i}{\partial m_i} > 0 \qquad \frac{\partial A_i}{\partial p_i} < 0 \qquad \frac{\partial A_i}{\partial w_i} > 0 \qquad \frac{\partial^2 A_i}{\partial w_i^2} < 0. \qquad (2.4)$$

2.3.2 Match attendance

One can also be interested in the variables that explain the attendance of an individual game. In this approach, beside the price, the size of the market and the winning percentage of the home team, other factors have to be taken into consideration. First of all, a distinction has to be made between the home and away games. It makes a difference if team x is playing against team y in the large home market of team x or in the small home market of team y.

An additional explanatory variable might be the winning percentage of the visiting team. On the one hand, referring to the uncertainty of outcome, the closeness between the two teams can have a positive effect on match attendance, so that the squared difference between the winning percentages matters. However, as mentioned above, this effect does not get much empirical support. On the other hand, fans love to watch their team playing against a top team, not only because it promises to be a high-quality game, but also because it is a thrill to see a moderate team beating a top team. The winning percentage of the visiting team can also be seen as an indicator of the absolute quality of the match.

One might also consider including the size of the market of the visiting team and the distance between the markets of the two teams. For instance, if the distance between the teams is not large, as in some small European countries, the visiting team can bring its own supporters. In the North American major leagues, however, its effect is less important. So, the demand function for tickets of a single game can be specified as:

$$A_{ij} = A_{ij}[m_i, m_j, dist_{ij}, w_i, w_j, p_i] \qquad \text{for all } i, j \, i \neq j, \qquad (2.5)$$

where A_{ij} is the number of spectators attending the game of home team i playing against visiting team j. The signs of market size, price and home winning percentage are the same as in (2.3); the market size and the winning percentage of the visiting team can be expected to have a positive effect on match attendance.

The relationship between season attendance and game attendance of all teams is then simply:

$$A_i = \sum_{j \neq i}^{n} A_{ij} \qquad \text{for all } i.$$

The estimation of this (indirect) specification of the season attendance function can yield more information than the (direct) specification of the season demand function in (2.3), but it also needs a considerably larger data set.

2.4   Club revenue and cost

Stadium attendances determine a club's gate receipts, which is simply the number of tickets sold multiplied by the average ticket price. The total season revenue of a modern sports club, however, does not depend only on ticket sales. Over the last few decades, the share of gate receipts in the budget of a club has diminished. Broadcasting rights and commercial income, such as sponsorship, merchandising and licensing, have gradually taken over. Nevertheless, there seems to be a positive correlation between the sum of commercial and broadcasting revenues, on the one hand, and stadium attendances, on the other hand. Sponsors, as well as the merchandising business, are more interested in successful clubs with many spectators. Also, television companies prefer to broadcast games that are watched by many people. If this positive correlation seems to be obvious for commercial revenue, it is less so for broadcast revenue. However, even if a broadcast game has a negative effect on stadium attendance, its greater exposure increases the clubs' commercial income. Moreover, empirical studies show that it is not very clear whether televised and live games are substitutes or complements (see Siegfried and Hinshaw, 1979; Simmons and Buraimo, 2005). So, in order to simplify the analysis, we assume in this model that the sum of all non-gate receipts of a club is proportional to the club's stadium attendance. The value of the proportionality factor can differ between clubs. The proportionality factor will also be different in each national league, depending on the size of the national market and the international reputation of the league. Whereas gate receipts are dominantly determined by the size of the local market, television rights, sponsoring and merchandising are rather determined by the size of the national market. If κ_i is the proportionality factor, the total season revenue of a club is then equal to the sum of gate receipts $p_i A_i$ and all other revenues $\kappa_i A_i$ and can be specified as:

$$R_i = (p_i + \kappa_i)A_i[m_i, w_i, p_i] = R_i[m_i, w_i, p_i] \qquad K_i > 0 \qquad (2.6)$$

Based on the conditions of the attendance function as given in (2.4), the following conditions hold for the revenue function:

$$\frac{\partial R_i}{\partial m_i} = (p + \kappa_i)\frac{\partial A_i}{\partial m_i} > 0$$

$$\frac{\partial R_i}{\partial w_i} = (p_i + \kappa_i)\frac{\partial A_i}{\partial w_i} > 0 \qquad\qquad (2.7)$$

$$\frac{\partial^2 R_i}{\partial w_i^2} = (p_i + \kappa_i)\frac{\partial^2 A_i}{\partial w_1^2} < 0.$$

The impact of a change in the ticket price on total season revenue is more complicated. A higher ticket price lowers attendance, but it increases the revenue per attendee. If revenue consists only of ticket sales, a well-known result from microeconomic theory is that the effect of the price change on revenue depends on the value of price elasticity of the demand for tickets. The price elasticity $\varepsilon_i = -\frac{\partial A_i}{\partial p_i}\frac{p_i}{A_i}$ is the ratio of the percentage change in attendance and the percentage change in the price. If the price elasticity is larger than one, the price has a negative effect on revenue; if the price elasticity is smaller than one, the price has a positive effect on revenue; if the price elasticity is equal to one, a price change has no effect on revenue.

If there are more revenue sources than just ticket sales, as in revenue function (2.6), the price effect can be calculated as:

$$\frac{\partial R_i}{\partial p_i} = A_i + (p_i + \kappa_i)\frac{\partial A_i}{\partial p_i} = A_i\left(1 - \varepsilon_i/\frac{p_i}{p_i + \kappa_i}\right).$$

From this expression it can be derived that the effect of the ticket price on total revenue is positive (negative) if the price elasticity is smaller (larger) than the share of gate receipts in team revenue ($\frac{p_i}{p_i + \kappa_i}$). This ratio is clearly smaller than one, and decreases with the importance of the non-gate receipts. If the non-gate receipts become the dominant revenue source, the ticket price will have a positive effect on club revenue only if the price elasticity of ticket demand is very low. This can be explained by the fact that a price increase will lower not only attendances, but also a club's broadcast and commercial revenue.

On the cost side of many clubs, the players or the playing talents are the most important factors of production, and the largest share of total season expenditures is spend on player salaries. There is obviously a close relationship between the talents of the team and its winning percentage, but this will be discussed in Chapter 3.

The player labour cost can be calculated as the number of a team's playing talents (not the number of players, as will be explained in Chapter 3) multiplied by the unit cost of talent. Besides the player salaries, club owners who also own their stadium face a considerable capital cost, which is a fixed cost in the short run. If all other cost elements are neglected in this model, the total season cost function of a club can simply be written as:

$$C_i = c_i t_i + c_i^0, \qquad (2.8)$$

where c_i^0 is the fixed capital cost and c_i the marginal unit cost of talent. If the player labour market is competitive, the market clearing cost of a unit of talent will be the same for every club, so that in (2.8) $c_i = c$ for all i. Vrooman (1995) introduced a more general cost function where the marginal cost of talent can be different for each team and where the market size can also affect the cost of talent. In the following chapters, however, we will use the simplified specification above. This specification of the cost function also implies that the marginal cost of spectators is zero, i.e. $\frac{\partial C_i}{\partial A_i} = 0$, which seems to be a plausible assumption. One more spectator in the stadium does not increase the total cost of the club in any significant way. So, the marginal cost is extremely small and will be put equal to zero in this model.

2.5 Ticket pricing

In most industries where many producers are competing to sell their products to many consumers, the price of the products is determined by the market. The law of demand and supply fixes the market clearing equilibrium price level. The question is whether this is also true in the professional team sports industry. One of the important consequences of leagues' regulations on the product market is that most clubs are local monopolists. Some exceptions exist in very large US cities or densely populated areas, or in Europe, where the relegation and promotion system can bring two clubs of the same city into the highest division. Fan loyalty in sports, however, makes the application of a duopoly model rather questionable.

From economic theory, we know that profit-maximising monopoly holders tend to increase prices above and reduce output below Pareto-optimum values. Whereas in a competitive product market firms are price takers, the single firm in a monopoly market is a price maker. As a local monopolist, a sports club faces the downward-sloping market demand curve for its tickets, so that it can set the ticket price at a level which realises its objective of profit or win maximisation.

To show the implications step by step, we will first consider a model where a club's only revenue is the sale of tickets, so that κ_i in revenue function (2.6) equals zero, and where the ticket price is the only decision variable, given a fixed number of talents. What will be the optimal ticket price if the club is a **profit maximiser**? Dropping the subscripts, the club's profit function can now be written as:

$$\pi = pA - C.$$

In order to find the optimal ticket price, the partial derivative of the profit function with respect to the ticket price has to equal zero:

$$\frac{\partial \pi}{\partial p} = p\frac{\partial A}{\partial p} + A = 0. \tag{2.9}$$

Because the marginal cost of spectators is assumed to be zero, a change in the ticket price does not affect the club's total cost. Applying the chain rule, and given that the marginal cost of spectators is zero:

$$\frac{\partial C}{\partial p} = \frac{\partial C}{\partial A}\frac{\partial A}{\partial p} = 0.$$

It follows that the profit maximisation condition is equivalent to the revenue maximisation condition. The optimal ticket price is found where:

$$\varepsilon = -\frac{\partial A}{\partial p}\frac{p}{A} = 1,$$

so that profits are maximised at the point where the price elasticity equals one.

Assuming that the demand function $A[m, p, w]$ can be drawn as a linear function of the ticket price, Figure 2.3 presents the downward-sloping demand curve. As can be derived, the price elasticity equals one in point E, exactly at the middle of the linear demand curve where $\frac{A}{p} = -\frac{\partial A}{\partial p}$. The optimal price is p_1 and A_1 spectators buy a ticket. At the upper (lower) part of the demand function, the price elasticity is larger (smaller) than one.

In fixing the optimal ticket price, it is possible that the club manager faces a **stadium capacity constraint**. The optimal ticket price, given a stadium capacity constraint, can now be found at the point of intersection of the

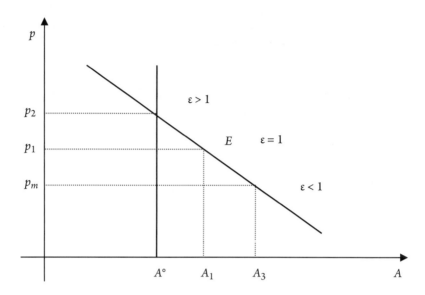

Figure 2.3 Demand for tickets

demand curve and the capacity constraint. If the stadium cannot receive more than A^0 spectators, as indicated in Figure 2.3, a profit-maximising owner will set the ticket price at p_2 above p_1.

We now extend the pricing model by also including the non-gate revenue and investigate if this changes the optimal ticket price. Because the cost is not affected by the ticket price, a profit-maximising club will set the ticket price that maximises total revenue:

$$\frac{\partial \pi}{\partial p} = \frac{\partial R}{\partial p} = (p + \kappa)\frac{\partial A}{\partial p} + A = 0 \quad \text{or} \quad \varepsilon = \frac{p}{p + \kappa} < 1. \quad (2.10)$$

It follows that the optimal ticket price is now set where the price elasticity is smaller than one. Given the same demand curve for tickets as depicted in Figure 2.3, the optimal ticket price is found in the inelastic part of the demand curve. A lower ticket price will be set compared with the price set in the model with only gate receipts. With a lower ticket price, stadium attendance will be higher, and so are all non-gate revenues that are proportional to attendance. It follows that profits will also be higher.

If most clubs in professional sports leagues are local monopolists on the product market, they are price makers and can set ticket prices above the social optimum level. League authorities, however, can impose **maximum**

ticket prices. How does a maximum ticket price affect club revenue? In Figure 2.3, the profit-maximising ticket price was given by p_1. If the league imposes a maximum ticket price of p_m, it is obvious that this increases attendance from A_1 to A_3, but it lowers a club's season revenue and profit.

An interesting question is how an increase in the cost of playing talent affects the optimal ticket price. Club owners often argue that player salaries should be under control in order to keep ticket prices low, so that low-income people can also afford to attend the games. This sounds reasonable. However, if clubs are local monopolists in the product market, trying to maximise profits, lower salaries will not lower the optimal ticket price. Solving the equations (2.9) and (2.10) for the optimal ticket price, it is clear that the cost of talent does not appear in this solution. So, a profit-maximising club will not change its ticket price if player salaries are lowered. Decreasing the unit cost of playing talent, with a constant number of playing talents, will only lower a club's total cost and increase its profits (see Noll, 1974c). As seen in Chapter 4, where the two-decision variable model is analysed, and also the number of talents hired by the club can be adjusted, a lower unit cost of talent will not lower but increase the profit-maximising ticket price.

What if clubs are **win maximisers**? Referring to the win-maximisation objective (1.2), the only way a club manager can maximise the winning percentage of his team is by hiring as many talents as he can afford within the limits of his budget. However, in this first version of the model, we have assumed that the number of talents is fixed and that the ticket price is the only decision variable. It follows that the win-maximisation model does not apply here. The ticket price decision of a win-maximising club will be addressed using a two-decision variable model in Chapter 4.

2.6   Sports and the media

It is not necessary to go to the ball park to watch a game. Sports have become very popular media products, in particular on television. Sports and television are very much in need of each other's company. In many countries, sports get the highest spectator ratings, and televised sports, being one of the channels for international companies and sponsors to market their products, have become the most important revenue source of private television companies. On the other hand, broadcasting rights and sponsorship have become the major revenue source of sports clubs and leagues. Nevertheless, this relationship between sports and the media has also raised many questions and problems (see Jeanrenaud and Késenne, 2006).

In analysing the relationship between sports and television, it is important to make a clear distinction between the upstream market of broadcast rights, where the clubs or the league is on the supply side and the television companies are on the demand side, and the downstream market of television sports, where the television companies are on the supply side and the spectators are on the demand side.

2.6.1 The market of broadcast rights

In all US major leagues, as well as in most national football leagues in Europe, the market of broadcast rights is monopolised by the league, and the revenues are distributed in one way or another among all clubs. In only a few countries, like Spain, Portugal and Greece, and also Italy until 2010, can football clubs individually sell the media rights of their home games. In Spain, the two largest and richest clubs, Real Madrid and FC Barcelona, sell their broadcast rights individually, while the other teams pool their rights and share the money among each other.

The leagues' argument for the monopolisation or the collective sale of broadcast rights is that the broadcasting rights have become such a dominant revenue source that the money has to be distributed among all teams in order to guarantee a reasonable competitive balance in the league. However, this is a false or a misleading argument, because the broadcast money can also be redistributed among all the teams without the monopolisation of the broadcast rights. The league can allow the individual sale of the rights of the home games by each team, and then tax the teams' media revenue and redistribute the collected money.

In the *White Paper on Sports* (Commission of the European Communities, 2007), it is stated that: 'While joint selling of media rights raises competition concerns, the Commission has accepted it under certain conditions. Collective selling can be important for the distribution of income and can be a tool for achieving greater solidarity within sports.' In my opinion, this is a very questionable statement. If the joint selling of media rights raises competition concerns, it should be banned, because collective selling is not important for the distribution of income, nor is it the best tool for achieving greater solidarity within sports.

Furthermore, Szymanski and Leach (2005) have shown in an empirical study that the competitive balance that emerges from a competitive player market without any regulation is more balanced than the public's revealed preference. Indeed the empirical evidence that the public turns away from unbalanced

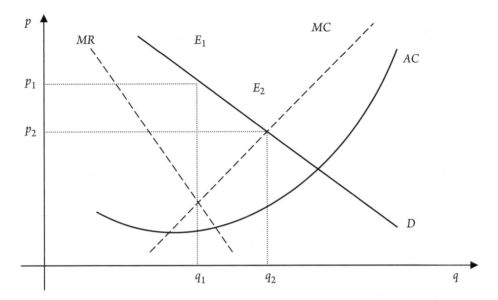

Figure 2.4 Monopoly versus perfect competition

championships is not very convincing (see Borland and Macdonald, 2003; Coates et al., 2012).

Moreover, microeconomic theory shows that, in monopolised markets, prices are too high and output is too low compared with competitive markets, which is shown in the well-known diagram of Figure 2.4. The profit-maximising point of the monopolist is given by E_1 at the point of intersection of the marginal revenue and the marginal cost curve. The competitive market equilibrium is given by E_2, where the market demand and supply curves intersect. The monopoly price is clearly higher and the monopoly output is lower.

Also, in some countries, the courts have called the pooling of television rights illegal, or in defiance of European competition laws. It is not the league or the sports federation but the clubs that are the legal owners of the broadcast rights of their home games.

Another argument in favour of the monopolisation of the broadcast rights is that the collective sale of TV rights will generate higher broadcast revenues. The individual sale of the rights by clubs would imply high transaction costs because of intensive bargaining between all clubs and all broadcasters for all games. The high transaction costs reduce the net revenue of decentralised selling. If one starts from a product market of matches that qualify to be televised, it is hard to see how decentralised selling could beat pooled selling in collecting broadcast revenues. The monopoly league's total cost of selling the TV rights includes only the (transaction) cost of bargaining between the league and the bidding broadcasters. It follows that the transaction costs are low and independent of the number of TV rights, so that the marginal cost is (close to) zero. With a given demand curve for TV rights, a profit-maximising sports federation will set the price and sell the number of broadcast rights that maximise revenue. It is obvious that this revenue can hardly be improved by a decentralised selling of the TV rights by individual clubs. However, games are not homogeneous products, because they are all of different quality. But if only the top games of the top teams, which are all of (an expected) top quality, are taken into account, this model can serve only as a first approximation and indication of the outcome. A more advanced analysis of the bidding process is needed to find out under which regime the highest broadcast revenue can be collected. It follows that a welfare economic analysis is necessary that includes the welfare losses of monopolisation, as well as the gains from higher broadcast revenues.

The collection and distribution of broadcast rights (*)

In the following model, we will examine which collection and distribution of broadcast rights is optimal in terms of improving the competitive balance without reducing the investments in talent in a win-maximisation league. We argue in this section that clubs should sell the broadcast rights of their home games individually in a competitive market of broadcast rights with many clubs on the supply side and many television companies on the demand side. But the league should tax the clubs' revenues and distribute the money among all teams. Késenne (2009a) has shown that, in a profit-maximisation league, decentralised selling of broadcast rights with performance-related revenue sharing is the best scenario to improve competitive balance.

Falconieri et al. (2004) investigated the welfare effects of collective versus individual sale of television rights, and conclude that collective sale is socially preferable if leagues are small and homogeneous, and if teams receive little performance-related revenue. However, Falconieri et al. (2004) do not consider the possibility that broadcasting money could be distributed if it had been collected individually by all the clubs.

In this section, the analysis concentrates only on the impact of selling and sharing broadcast rights on competitive balance and talent investment, because the need for a reasonable competitive balance in a sports league has always been one of the main arguments to justify the monopolisation of media rights. However, an extensive empirical study by Thomas Peeters (2011) has shown that there is no significant connection between the monopolisation of media rights and the competitive balance in the national European football leagues.

If one wants to analyse the impact of pooling and sharing broadcast rights, the starting point is the benchmark case of a non-pooling/non-sharing equilibrium, without any league intervention. Our analysis uses a simple two-club Nash equilibrium model where the demand for talent or the talent investment is the only decision variable. Four different scenarios are compared regarding the selling of broadcasting rights and the distribution of the rights among the clubs, and the impact on talent investment and competitive balance.

Assume a two-club league, with x being the large-market club and y the small-market club. Each club has two basic sources of season revenue: gate receipts and media rights. We assume that gate receipts are determined simply by the product of the size of the market (m_i) and the win percentage (w_i).

We further assume that the media revenue of each club, in the benchmark case, is proportional to the gate receipts, with a larger proportionality factor (κ_i) in the large-market club. See Garcia and Rodriguez (2002) and Forrest and Simmons (2006) for empirical evidence on the relationship between broadcasting and gate attendances in Spain's La Liga and the English Premier League, respectively. For simplicity reasons, we also assume that televising games does not affect gate receipts.

In the benchmark case, the sale of broadcast rights is decentralised, without any sharing or other league intervention. So, if R_i is a club's total season revenue, the revenue functions of the large- and the small-market club can be written as:

$$R_x = (1 + \kappa_x) m_x w_x \ or \ R_x = (1 + \kappa_x) \sigma w_x \ with \ \sigma = m_x / m_y$$

$$R_y = (1 + \kappa_y) m_y w_y \ or \ R_y = (1 + \kappa_y) w_y \ and \ m_x > m_y \ and \ \kappa_x > \kappa_y. \quad (2.11)$$

The season winning percentage of a team depends on its relative playing strength, where the number of talents in a team, not the number of players, is given by t_i:

$$w_x = \frac{t_x}{t_x + t_y}, w_y = \frac{t_y}{t_x + t_y}.$$

Club revenue functions are linear in winning percentage but concave in talent. The supply of talent in the league $(t_x + t_y)$ is assumed to be flexible, as it is in the win-maximising and the open national football leagues in Europe.

On the cost side, we consider only a variable player cost and a capital cost that is fixed in the short run, so the total cost can be written as:

$$C_i = ct_i + c_i^0 \quad i: x, y,$$

where c is the equilibrium unit cost of talent in a competitive player market where all teams are wage takers.

In this approach, we assume that all clubs, at the start of the season, decide on the quantity of talent, with an exogenously given unit cost of talent. In this non-cooperative **Nash equilibrium** model, the winning percentage of one team also depends on the talent employed by the other team.

If all teams are win maximisers, they will maximise their winning percentage under the breakeven constraint: $R_i = ct_i + c_i^0$ with $c_i^0 = kR_i$ so that $(1 - k)R_i = ct_i$.

This specification implies that all teams have the same wage/turnover ratio $(1 - k)$.

In that scenario, it can be derived that, in the benchmark model without any league intervention, the competitive balance is given by:

$$\frac{w_x}{w_y} = \frac{t_x}{t_y} = \frac{(1 - k)cR_x}{(1 - k)cR_y} = \frac{R_x}{R_y}.$$

The team with the larger budget will be the more talented and successful team. Therefore, competitive balance will be improved if the percentage increase of the small team's revenue is larger than the percentage increase of the large team's revenue.

Starting from the benchmark case above, different scenarios regarding the selling and distribution of broadcast rights can be distinguished:

1. centralised selling and equal sharing;
2. centralised selling and performance-related sharing;
3. decentralised selling and equal sharing;
4. decentralised selling and performance-related sharing.

We will consider these scenarios in turn and compare their impact on competitive balance and investment in talent.

1. In the case of centralised selling and equal sharing of the collected media rights, the total revenue of each team after sharing, indicated by the superscript *, is then:

$$R^*_x = \sigma w_x + v/2 \qquad R^*_y = w_y + v/2,$$

where v is the total media revenue of the league.

The percentage change in club revenue can be seen to be:

$$\Delta R_x / R_x = \frac{R^*_x - R_x}{R_x} = \frac{v/2 - \kappa_x \sigma w_x}{(1 + \kappa_x) \sigma w_x}$$

$$\Delta R_y / R_y = \frac{R^*_y - R_y}{R_y} = \frac{v/2 - \kappa_y w_y}{(1 + \kappa_y) w_y} > 0.$$

The revenue of the small-market team will increase; it receives 50 per cent of the total media rights, but it would not be able to raise so much money on its own. The revenue of the large-market team can go up or down, because the amount of broadcast money is assumed to be higher in the centralised than in the decentralised case. However, one can conclude that the competitive balance will improve. The total investment in talent will be higher because $v > \kappa_x \sigma w_x + \kappa_y w_y$.

2. If the centralised media money (v) is distributed depending on team performance, or the winning percentages of the teams, team revenue after sharing will be:

$$R^*_x = \sigma w_x + w_x v \qquad R^*_y = w_y + w_y v.$$

The changes in teams' revenues are:

$$\Delta R_x / R_x = \frac{R^*_x - R_x}{R_x} = \frac{w_x v - \kappa_x \sigma w_x}{(1 + \kappa_x) \sigma w_x}$$

$$\Delta R_y / R_y = \frac{R^*_y - R_y}{R_y} = \frac{w_y v - \kappa_y w_y}{(1 + \kappa_y) w_y}.$$

The result will be an improvement in competitive balance because:

$$\frac{v - \kappa_x \sigma}{(1 + \kappa_x)\sigma} < \frac{v - \kappa_y}{(1 + \kappa_y)}.$$

The percentage change in the small-market team's revenue is larger than the percentage change in the large-market team's revenue.

Again, the total investment in talent will increase if $v > b_x \sigma w_x + b_y w_y$.

3. In the case of decentralised selling of the broadcast rights, the league is taxing the media revenue of the teams with an average tax rate of α. If the tax receipts of the league are equally distributed among the teams, the teams' revenues after sharing are:

$$R_x^* = \sigma w_x + (1 - \alpha)\kappa_x \sigma w_x + \alpha(\kappa_x \sigma w_x + \kappa_y w_y)/2$$

$$R_y^* = w_y + (1 - \alpha)\kappa_y w_y + \alpha(\kappa_x \sigma w_x + \kappa_y w_y)/2.$$

The percentage changes in club revenue are now:

$$\Delta R_x / R_x = \frac{R_x^* - R_x}{R_x} = \frac{\alpha \kappa_y w_y - \alpha \kappa_x \sigma w_x}{2(1 + \kappa_x)\sigma w_x} < 0$$

$$\Delta R_y / R_y = \frac{R_y^* - R_y}{R_y} = \frac{\alpha \kappa_x \sigma w_x - \alpha \kappa_y w_y}{2(1 + \kappa_y)w_y} > 0. \tag{2.12}$$

Clearly, competitive balance improves, and total talent investment does not change, which can be seen by summing the numerators of (2.12).

4. Finally, with decentralised selling of the rights, and performance-related distribution of the league's tax receipts, the after-sharing revenues of the teams are:

$$R_x^* = \sigma w_x + (1 - \alpha)\kappa_x \sigma w_x + w_x \alpha(\kappa_x \sigma w_x + \kappa_y w_y)$$

$$R_y^* = w_y + (1 - \alpha)\kappa_y w_y + w_y \alpha(\kappa_x \sigma w_x + \kappa_y w_y).$$

The percentage changes in team revenue are:

$$\Delta R_x / R_x = \frac{R_x^* - R_x}{R_x} = \frac{(\alpha \kappa_x \sigma w_x + \alpha \kappa_y w_y - \alpha \kappa_x \sigma)}{(1 + \kappa_x)\sigma} < 0$$

$$\Delta R_y / R_y = \frac{R_y^* - R_y}{R_y} = \frac{(\alpha \kappa_x \sigma w_x + \alpha \kappa_y w_y - \alpha \kappa_y)}{(1 + \kappa_y)} > 0.$$

Given that $w_x + w_y = 1$, these changes in revenue can be rewritten as:

$$\Delta R_x / R_x = \frac{aw_y(by - b_x\sigma)}{(1 + b_x)\sigma} < 0$$

$$\Delta R_y / R_y = \frac{aw_x(b_x\sigma - b_y)}{(1 + b_y)} > 0.$$

It is clear that the competitive balance will improve without changing total investment in talent. But the improvement in competitive balance is stronger under equal sharing, because $w_y < 1/2 < w_x$.

As distinct from the profit-maximisation case, the conclusion under win maximisation is that, even if all four scenarios improve the competitive balance without reducing total investment in talent, the individual selling of media rights, with equal sharing of the media revenue, is the best way to improve the competitive balance. However, teams may be better off with the monopolisation of the market of TV rights, because it can be expected that the total media revenue collected in a monopolised market will be higher than the sum of the revenues raised by the teams individually in a competitive market. Moreover, the transaction costs of an intensive decentralised bargaining process between all teams and all broadcasters may be higher (see Andreff and Bourg, 2006). To the extent that additional revenue increases the absolute quality of the games, there is a further gain for spectators. But a more important advantage for spectators from decentralised selling is that it does not cause the welfare loss that is expected in a monopolised market, with the prices of watching televised games set too high, and the number of televised games too low. What is good for clubs and the league is not necessarily good for spectators. A welfare economics approach is appropriate to find the optimal arrangement.

Obviously, the sharing and selling of broadcast rights in the North American major leagues and the national football leagues in Europe follow more complicated lines than any of the four extreme scenarios in our simplified model.

In the US major leagues, the national media rights are monopolised by the league and equally distributed among the teams (= scenario 1).

In most national football leagues in Europe, the media rights are also monopolised, with, at least partly, a performance-related distribution of the money (= +/− scenario 2).

An additional disadvantage of monopolising the broadcast rights is that, in most cases, the rights are sold as a package to just one broadcaster, so that a new monopoly is created in the downstream market of televised sports. If pay-per-view is an option, the price can again be too high and the output too low, compared with a more competitive market. Higher prices and less output will lower the spectators' real income and welfare.

Moreover, in many countries, it is argued that a national pastime, such as baseball in the US or football in Europe, should be broadcast free-to-air and cannot be hidden behind an expensive decoder, because it shows characteristics of a public good.

2.6.2 The market of televised sport

One of the questions concerns the demand for televised sport. Sports on television can be seen at home, lying on a relaxing couch in a warm and comfortable living room. In general, television spectators of a game are a different public from the diehard supporters of a team attending the game in the stadium (see Buraimo and Simmons, 2009). Television spectators are probably more interested in watching good play without being supporters of one of the teams. In the case of free-to-air television, the additional price, or the marginal cost, of watching a game on television is very low. In the case of a pay channel, or pay-per-view, the price can be high. This raises the question to what extent live sport and television sport are substitutes or complements. The answer can be given only by empirical research. Apart from the complications raised by delayed TV coverage or by broadcasting only the highlights of a game, the theoretical set-up of this research, as well as the specification of the demand function, is crucial for the interpretation of the results. It is obvious, for instance, that the number of spectators of a particular game can hardly be higher if that game is broadcast live. So, a dummy variable as an additional explanatory variable in attendance function (2.3), with the value of one if the game is broadcast, will probably yield a negative coefficient. Does it mean that stadium sport and television sport are substitutes? If season attendance is investigated, it is perfectly possible that a sport will become more popular because it is broadcast, so that more spectators are interested in experiencing it live. A good illustration of this phenomenon is that some less popular sport disciplines have to pay, and are willing to pay, to be televised instead of being paid. The more conventional way to test whether products are substitutes or complements is to estimate the cross-price elasticity. If the price of watching sports on television (p_{tv}) is added as an explanatory variable in demand curve (2.3), the answer depends on the sign of the price effect:

$$\frac{\partial A[m, w, p, p_{tv}]}{\partial p_{tv}}.$$

If this price effect is positive, televised sport and stadium sport are substitutes; if it is negative, they are complements.

Even if broadcasting more games reduces stadium attendance, it is still possible that more broadcasting will increase club revenue, because the loss of stadium attendance can be more than compensated for by the increase of broadcast rights.

Is pay TV more profitable than free TV?

The question that is dealt with in the model below is whether a profit-maximising television company that is granted the exclusive broadcast rights of a game or the whole championship will choose pay-per-view or free-to-air. Dietl and Hasan (2007) have shown that the probability of free TV airing major sports increases with, among other parameters, a higher sensitivity of sponsoring fees to viewer ratings and a higher price sensitivity of consumer demand.

In our model, we assume that a private and profit-maximising broadcaster has managed to get the exclusive rights to broadcast all the games, and has to choose between pay-per-view and free-to-air broadcasting (see also van der Burg, 1996).

A TV company has at least two revenue sources. As a monopolist, it is facing a downward-sloping market demand curve for pay-per-view sport, but the television company is also collecting money from advertising. Before, during and after the match, paid advertising can be inserted. The more spectators are expected to watch, the more advertisers are willing to pay, so that advertising revenue can be considered to be a positive function of the number of spectators.

On the cost side, there are, beside the cost of the broadcast rights, the operational costs of equipment, transportation and personnel. Both these cost categories are independent of the number of spectators, so that the marginal cost is zero. The more spectators, however, the lower the average cost will be.

Assume that the demand for TV sports, supplied by a monopolist broadcaster, is given by:

$$p = \alpha - \beta q,$$

where p is the price per view (or the subscription fee) and q is the number of spectators or the number of subscribers.

The smaller β, the more price elastic is the demand for TV sports. However, pay TV is not the broadcaster's only source of revenue. Besides the payments by TV spectators, a broadcaster can also receive income from TV advertising before, during or after the games. Assume that advertisers are willing to pay an amount as large as λ per TV viewer. It follows that the broadcaster's total revenue can be written as:

$$R = pq + \lambda q = (\alpha + \lambda)q - \beta q^2.$$

The average revenue per spectator AR is then: $R/q = p + \lambda = (\alpha + \lambda) - \beta q$, which is parallel to the demand curve D. The marginal revenue MR is:

$$\frac{\partial R}{\partial q} = (\alpha + \lambda) - 2\beta q.$$

On the cost side, we consider two cost categories: the broadcast rights the TV company has to pay, and the operational cost to broadcast the games, including transportation, equipment and personnel. These costs are all independent of the number of spectators who watch the games on TV. So the total cost $C = C_0$ is fixed, and the marginal cost is zero (see Késenne, 2012). In Figure 2.5 this model is presented graphically.

On the horizontal axis the number of spectators is measured, and on the vertical axis the pay-per-view price or the subscription fee. The demand for TV sport is presented by the linear curve D. Given that the average revenue (λ) from TV advertising is constant, the broadcaster's average and marginal revenue curves are given by AR and MR. Because the total cost is constant, the marginal cost is zero and the average cost is indicated by the downward-sloping hyperbolic curve AC.

If the pay TV broadcaster is a profit maximiser, he will set a price that maximises profits $\pi_p = R - C = (\alpha + \lambda)q - \beta q^2 - C_0$. From the first-order condition $(\alpha + \lambda) - 2\beta q = 0$, the optimal number of spectators can be found as $q^* = \frac{\alpha + \lambda}{2\beta}$.

The optimal price is then $p^* = \dfrac{\alpha - \lambda}{2}$.

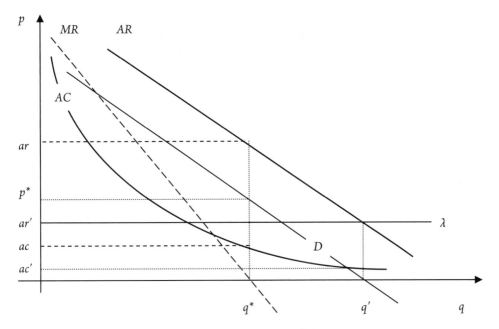

Figure 2.5 Pay-per-view versus free-to-air

From this result, it can be seen that the optimal price can be negative if $\alpha < \lambda$, although this outcome is not very realistic. It would imply that broadcasters are willing to pay their TV viewers, because sponsors are very sensitive to viewer ratings. Substituting the optimal values in the profit function, the broadcaster's profit in the pay TV scenario is then:

$$\pi_p^* = (\alpha + \lambda)\frac{(\alpha + \lambda)}{2\beta} - \beta\frac{(\alpha + \lambda)^2}{4\beta^2} - C_0 = \frac{(\alpha + \lambda)^2}{4\beta} - C_0.$$

In the free TV scenario with zero price $p' = 0$, the demand for games or the number of spectators would be $q' = \frac{\alpha}{\beta}$. Profit would then be equal to:

$$\pi_f^* = (\alpha + \lambda)\frac{\alpha}{\beta} - \beta\frac{\alpha^2}{\beta^2} - C_0 = \frac{\alpha\lambda}{\beta} - C_0.$$

The difference between the profits in both cases can then be calculated as:

$$\pi_p^* - \pi_f^* = \frac{(\alpha + \lambda)^2}{4\beta} - \frac{\alpha\lambda}{\beta} = \frac{(\alpha - \lambda)^2}{4\beta} > 0.$$

Because the difference is always positive, we can conclude that, for whatever values of the parameters α, β and λ, pay TV is more profitable, which confirms the general belief.

In Figure 2.5 the profit-maximising number of spectators is found at the point of intersection of the MR and the zero MC, which is q^*, and the optimal price is p^*. Profits can be found as the product of the number of spectators (q') and the difference between the average revenue (ar) and the average cost (ac).

In the free-to-air scenario with the price equal to zero, the number of spectators can be seen to equal q'. The average revenue (ar'), which now consists only of advertising receipts, is equal to λ. Profits are now indicated by the product of the number of spectators (q') and the difference between λ and the average cost (ac'). The difference in profits will be larger, the higher the demand level (α) and the more elastic the demand curve $(1/\beta)$. The more advertisers are willing to pay for TV advertising (λ), the lower will be the difference in profits.

Introducing board and shirt advertising (*)

The result in the previous section is not the end of story. If the games are broadcast free-to-air, more spectators watch, making it more interesting for businesses to advertise on players' shirts and field boards, which is an additional revenue to the organiser, the league or the club. Under these circumstances, the organiser would be willing to sell the broadcast rights at a lower price. The price reduction the organiser is willing to grant to a free-to-air broadcaster will depend on the extra TV spectators who can be expected on free TV compared with pay TV, which is in our model:

$$\Delta q = \frac{\alpha}{\beta} - \frac{\alpha + \lambda}{2\beta} = \frac{\alpha - \lambda}{2\beta}.$$

If these shirt and board advertisers are willing to pay the same amount of λ per viewer as paid by the TV advertiser, the reduced cost of the broadcaster will be:

$$C = C_0 - \lambda \frac{\alpha - \lambda}{2\beta}.$$

With this new cost function, with again a zero marginal cost, the difference between profits in the pay TV and the free TV cases becomes:

$$\pi_p - \pi_f = \frac{(\alpha - \lambda)^2}{4\beta} - \lambda \frac{(\alpha - \lambda)}{2\beta} = \frac{(\alpha - \lambda)}{4\beta}(\alpha - 3\lambda).$$

As can be seen now, $\pi_p < \pi_f$ if $\alpha/\lambda < 3$. So, it is not generally true that pay TV is more profitable than free TV. Free-to-air broadcasting can be more profitable than pay TV, depending on the ratio $\frac{\alpha}{\lambda}$, that is, depending on the level of demand and the price that advertisers are willing to pay per TV viewer. The lower the demand for televised sport and the more advertisers are willing to pay, the more profitable free TV will be. As distinct from the result in Dietl and Hasan (2007), the elasticity of the spectators' demand does not affect the choice for free TV.

In Figure 2.5, the impact of shirt and board advertising can be introduced by a downward shift of the average cost curve in the case of free TV, so that it is possible that free TV profits can be higher than pay TV profits.

One can take the analysis one step further by assuming that the marketing impact of a direct TV advertisement, which can show a video with a story or a clear message, is more effective than the impact of just a brand name on a board or a shirt. So, the money that advertisers are willing to pay per viewer is lower for board and shirt advertising. Assume that the price which advertisers are willing to pay per spectator for board and shirt advertising is: γ *with* $\gamma < \lambda$. In that case one can derive for the difference in profits:

$$\pi_p^* - \pi_f^* = \frac{(\alpha - \lambda)^2}{4\beta} - \gamma \frac{(\alpha - \lambda)}{2\beta} = \frac{(\alpha - \lambda)}{4\beta}(\alpha - \lambda - 2\gamma).$$

This implies that free TV is more profitable than pay TV if $\frac{\alpha - \lambda}{\gamma} < 2$, which is less likely than the previous condition $\alpha/\lambda < 3$. One might also consider including in the analysis the fact that many spectators do not like interruptions for TV advertising. If TV advertisements reduce the demand for televised sports, this implies a lower value of α, which makes it more likely that free TV is more profitable than pay TV.

Can this result also explain why, in the US major league sports, free TV prevails while, in European soccer, pay TV is more dominant? In other words, are there reasons to believe that the ratio between demand level and sponsor's sensitivity (α/λ) tends to be lower in the US and higher in Europe? Apart from historical, structural and institutional differences on both sides of the Atlantic (see Hoehn and Lancefield, 2003; Szymanski, 2003), an important factor is the scale effect in the US, with its large market compared to the smaller national markets in European soccer. However, in the US, four major leagues, with partly overlapping seasons, have to compete for TV spectators' interest, whereas in most European countries soccer is so dominant that there is hardly any competition from other televised sports. Moreover, as argued by Dietl and Hasan (2007), the average season appeal for games in Europe might be higher because of the promotion and relegation system, forcing the weaker teams to fight in order not to be relegated to a lower division, and because of the fight to qualify for the European competitions (UEFA Champions League and Europa League), which provide an additional contest in the national championships, possibly leading to a high demand for televised soccer in Europe. In our model above, the demand level is given by the size of the parameter α. We can think of only one reason why the value of λ, that is, the price advertisers are willing to pay per TV viewer, should be higher in the US than in Europe. Soccer in Europe goes on uninterrupted for two halves of 45 minutes each. The major league sports in the US, such as basketball, football and baseball, are interrupted more often, by time-outs and by their segmentation into thirds, quarters or ninths, which allows networks to run more commercials. So, the relative size of these parameters might be part of the explanation why the major league sports in the US are broadcast free-to-air and Europe has to pay to watch soccer on TV (see Késenne, 2012).

EXERCISES 2

2.1 Assume that gate receipts are a club's only source of revenue and that the demand function for tickets is given by $A = 5 - 0.5p$. The cost function is $C = 2t$. Attendances are measured in 10 000 fans and prices are in euros.

- What will be the optimal ticket price, the number of spectators and the total revenue of a profit-maximising club?
- Assume that the stadium can receive only 20 000 spectators. What will be the optimal ticket price and total revenue?

2.2 For the same club as in exercise 2.1, and assuming other revenues besides gate receipts, but proportional to attendances with proportionality factor $\kappa = 4$, derive the optimal ticket price, the number of spectators and total club revenue with and without the stadium capacity constraint that the maximum number of spectators is 20 000.

2.3 For the same club as in exercise 2.2, and assuming that the league is imposing a maximum ticket price of 2 euros, what will be the number of spectators and the club's revenue?

2.4 In a profit-maximising club with gate receipts as the only revenue source, the demand function for stadium tickets is given by $A = 5 - 0.5p$. Let the cost of talent be given by $C = ct$ with $t = 4$. Calculate the club's profit for different ticket prices, ranging from 3 to 7, and for different unit costs of talent, ranging from 2 to 4. What do you observe with respect to the relationship between the cost of talent and the profit-maximising ticket price?

2.5 Assume that the TV companies' demand curve for broadcast rights is given by $p_r = 12 - 2q_r$. If the total cost is fixed at $C = 3$, what will be the optimal price, the quantity sold and the profit of a monopoly league that is pooling the TV rights and tries to maximise profits?

2.6 With the same demand and cost function as in exercise 2.5, what will be the optimal price, quantity and revenue in a competitive market if the total cost function is given by $C = 2 + 0.2q_r^2$? Compare the results with the results of exercise 2.5. What do you conclude?

2.7 Assume that a broadcasting company's revenue consists of pay-per-view and advertising. Advertising revenue is given by $R_a = 4q_s$, and the demand for televised sport is $p_s = 10 - 0.5q_s$. The cost of the television company, consisting of TV rights and operational costs to broadcast the games, is fixed at $C = 50$. Without board or shirt advertising, will a profit-maximising TV company choose pay-per-view or free-to-air?

Appendix

The optimal competitive balance in a sports league

In this appendix, we try to derive theoretically what the optimal competitive balance in a league is from a welfare economic point of view, based on the most important parameters that can affect this optimum. First, the optimal winning percentage is derived for one particular team. Then, using a simple welfare function, we try to derive the social optimum.

The optimal winning percentage of a team

Among the most important variables affecting attendance, apart from the absolute quality of the league and the ticket price, which are exogenously determined in this analysis, are the size of the market and the winning percentage of the team. Teams with a high drawing potential, in large markets or densely populated areas, attract more spectators than teams with a limited drawing potential in small towns. But the empirical research also shows that spectators prefer a winning home team and that they turn away from a losing home team. However, if some degree of uncertainty of outcome is necessary in sports, the question is whether an optimal competitive balance can be derived, taking into account the interest of all supporters and spectators.

In order to analyse this, we start from a simplified two-team league with one large-market team x and one small-market team y, so $m_x > m_y$. The utility function of the supporters of both teams, with a given market size, depends on the team's winning percentage (w) and on the uncertainty of outcome (uo) in the league, which is measured in its most simple way by:

$$uo = w_x w_y.$$

Indeed, this indicator is zero if $w_i = 0$ and if $w_i = 1$, and it reaches its highest value for $w_i = 0.5$. Assuming that the utility function of the supporters of a team can be approached by the weighted product of the winning percentage and the uncertainty of outcome, this can be written for a two-team league as:

$$U_x = w_x^{1-\alpha} uo^\alpha = w_x w_y^\alpha \qquad \text{with } 0 \le \alpha \le 1$$

$$U_y = w_y^{1-\beta} uo^\beta = w_y w_x^\beta \qquad \text{with } 0 \le \beta \le 1.$$

The weights α and β are assumed to be different in the two teams, because it is reasonable to assume that the supporters of a strong large-market team value winning and competitive balance differently to the supporters of a weak small-market team.

Based on these utility functions, one can derive the optimal winning percentage for both teams from the first-order condition $\frac{\partial U_i}{\partial w_i} = 0$ as:

$$\frac{\partial U_x}{\partial w_x} = w_y^\alpha - \alpha w_x w_y^{\alpha-1} = 0$$

$$\frac{\partial U_y}{\partial w_y} = w_x^\beta - \beta w_y w_x^{\beta-1} = 0$$

or after some rearrangement:

$$w_y^{\alpha-1}(w_y - \alpha w_x) = 0$$

$$w_x^{\beta-1}[(w_x - \beta w_y) = 0.$$

Because $w_y^{\alpha-1}$ *and* $w_x^{\beta-1}$ are both different from zero, we can derive that the optimal competitive balance for the supporters of both teams is:

$$w_x/w_y = 1/\alpha$$

$$w_y/w_x = 1/\beta.$$

So, if $\alpha = \beta = 0.5$, the optimal winning percentage the supporters prefer for their home team can be found to be:

$$\frac{w_x}{w_y} = 2 \, or \, w_x^* = 2/3 = 0.67$$

$$\frac{w_y}{w_x} = 2 \, or \, w_y^* = 2/3 = 0.67.$$

The more the supporters value winning (that is, the smaller is α *and* β), the higher the optimal winning percentage of their home team will be. It is obvious that both teams prefer a winning percentage that is larger than 0.5, but this is impossible because the sum of the winning percentages in a two-team league has to equal unity.

The optimal competitive balance

In order to find the optimal competitive balance from a welfare economic point of view, we need to specify a welfare function which could be the weighted product of the utilities of the supporters of the large- and small-market team:

$$W = U_x^{m_x} U_y^{m_y} U_n^{m_n} = U_x^m U_y U_n^n,$$

where the weight m equals the ratio of the market sizes, because a large-market team has more supporters than a small-market team, so $m = \frac{m_x}{m_y} > 1$. We have also added a third utility function of the neutral TV spectators, which is:

$$U_n = uo = w_x w_y. \tag{2A.1}$$

Assuming that the neutral spectators are not supporters of one of the teams, the winning percentage of one of the teams does not matter; the utility of the neutral supporters is determined only by the uncertainty of outcome; its weight in the welfare function is given by the parameter n, which equals the ratio of the number of neutral (television) spectators m_n and the number of supporters of the small market team (m_y).

So, we can derive that:

$$W = U_x^m U_y U_n^n = (w_x w_y^\alpha)^m (w_y w_x^\beta)(w_x w_y)^n = w_x^{m+\beta+n} w_y^{\alpha m+n+1}.$$

The first-order condition for the optimal winning percentage of the large-market team x can be found as:

$$\frac{\partial W}{\partial w_x} = (m+\beta+\gamma) w_x^{m+\beta+n-1} w_y^{\alpha m+n+1} - (\alpha m+\gamma+1) w_y^{\alpha m+n} w_x^{m+\beta+n} = 0,$$

which, after some rearrangement, can be written as:

$$w_y^{\alpha m+n} w_x^{m+\beta+n-1} [m+\beta+n) w_y - (\alpha m+n+1) w_x] = 0.$$

Because the product before the parentheses is non-zero, the expression between the parentheses has to equal zero. So, we can find that the optimal competitive balance is:

$$\frac{w_x}{w_y} = \frac{m+\beta+n}{\alpha m+1+n}.$$

Based on these simple utility and welfare functions, we can derive that the optimal competitive balance depends on the preferences of the supporters of the large- and the small-market team, on the relative size of the markets of the two clubs, and on the number of neutral spectators or the importance of televised sport. One can also derive from (2A.1) that:

$$\frac{\partial(w_x/w_y)}{\partial m} > 0 \quad and \quad \frac{\partial(w_x/w_y)}{\partial \beta} > 0 \quad and \quad \frac{\partial(w_x/w_y)}{\partial \alpha} < 0.$$

The larger the market of a team, the higher will be the optimal winning percentage of that team. The more supporters value a winning team, the higher the optimal winning percentage of that team.

Also, it does not come as a surprise that, if $m = 1$ *and* $\alpha = \beta$, for whatever value of n, that is, the size of the group of neutral supporters, we find that both teams should have the same winning percentage $(\frac{w_x}{w_y} = 1)$.

More interesting is the result that even a very large difference in market size or drawing potential does not justify strong large-team dominance in the league. Indeed:

$$\lim_{m \to \infty} \frac{w_x}{w_y} = \lim_{m \to \infty} \frac{m + \beta + n}{\alpha m + 1 + n} = 1/\alpha.$$

So, if $\alpha = 0.5$, that is, the supporters of the large-market team value winning and uncertainty of outcome equally, whatever the difference between the market sizes of the teams in a league, and whatever the preferences of the small-market team supporters, the optimal competitive balance should always stay below 2, which implies that on no account should the optimal winning percentage of a large-market team be larger than $w_x = 0.67$.

Only if the supporters of the large-market team show a strong preference for winning, relative to uncertainty of outcome, can the optimal competition be very unbalanced.

Large differences in preferences for winning between the supporters of two teams with the same market size also do not strongly affect the optimal competitive balance. The winning percentage of the large-market team should again not be larger than $w_x = 0.67$.

Furthermore, it can be derived from the optimal competitive balance (2A.2) that:

$$\frac{\partial(w_x/w_y)}{\partial n} = \frac{(\alpha m + 1 + n) - (m + \beta + n)}{(\alpha m + 1 + n)^2} < 0 \quad for \ w_x > w_y. \qquad (2A.2)$$

It follows that the larger the group of more neutral television spectators becomes, the more balanced the competition should be from a welfare economic perspective.

3

Player labour market

3.1 Introduction

The players are the most important production factor and labour input in the industry of professional team sports. Other labour inputs come from coaches, youth trainers, maintenance workers, managers and so on. In this chapter we consider only the input of playing talent. The peculiar economics of the professional team sports industry has inspired league administrators to interfere not only in the product market but also in the player labour market. Their major concern has always been the competitive balance in the league and the top players' salary. The argument goes that a free and competitive player market will lead to a concentration of all playing talents in the rich large-market clubs. A rich club can afford to offer the best players a higher salary and, if they are free to move, the best players will play for the best-paying teams. This will result in a championship with a low uncertainty of outcome. Another concern has been the bidding up of top player salaries in the clubs' rat race for the best players in a competitive market, which can cause serious financial problems in many clubs.

In the past, the most important league regulation of the player market was the restriction on the free movement of players. The so-called Reserve Clause in the USA, which was lifted in the mid-1970s, and the so-called (retain-and-)transfer system in Europe, which was abolished in the mid-1990s, did not allow players to change teams at the end of their contract. The abolition of these restrictions has certainly made the player labour market more competitive. Other regulations that can seriously affect player salaries and the distribution of talent among teams are the rookie draft, revenue-sharing arrangements and salary caps. In all the sections of this chapter, except the one on player market segmentation, we will study the labour market in terms of the number of playing talents and not the number of players. One obvious reason is that in all team sports the number of players who can be fielded is fixed or, as in many sports, the league fixes the (maximum) number of players on the roster. Another reason is that players are very heterogeneous; there are top players and there are more moderate players. Top players have many playing talents; moderate players are less talented. In order to have a homogeneous labour input, we deal with playing talents so that the wage rate or the salary level is the unit cost of talent. A player with many talents is better paid and costs more than a player with few talents. This approach has its disadvantages as well, apart from the fact that the empirical implementation is problematic. The same number of playing talents in a football club can hide a totally different playing strength of the team. A football club with 100 talents that are equally distributed over the 25 players on the roster, so each player has only four talents, can field a team of only $11 \times 4 = 44$ talents. Another club that also has 100 talents, but with the 11 best players having eight talents each, can field a team of 88 talents. The latter team will be twice as strong as the former, although both clubs have 100 talents.

In this chapter, the functioning of the player market will be investigated, under both the profit- and the win-maximisation hypotheses. After a discussion of the demand and the supply on the talent market, we will analyse different models based on different assumptions regarding the club objectives and the supply of talent.

3.2   Demand and supply of talent

From microeconomic theory, we know that the market supply curve of labour is an upward-sloping function of the wage rate and, as in most labour markets of high-skilled workers, the short-term wage elasticity of labour supply is very low. Because professional players are highly skilled and well trained, we can make the simplifying assumption, without much loss of generality, that, in a league with a closed labour market, the supply of talent is constant in the short run. The player markets of the North American major leagues can be considered as closed markets. The national football leagues of most European countries, however, have been operating in an open EU player market since the Bosman verdict (European Court of Justice, 1995). This market cannot be approached by a fixed-supply model, because clubs can hire talents from other countries, even mid-season, which changes the supply of talent in the national leagues.

The season revenue function of a club that is concave in the winning percentage was defined in (2.6) as:

$$R_i = R_i[m_i, w_i, p_i]. \tag{3.1}$$

The market size of a team is not a decision variable in this model, and in this chapter, which concentrates on the player labour market, the ticket price is assumed to be constant. Also the winning percentage of a team cannot be controlled by the team owner. Although he can try to increase his team's winning percentage by hiring more talents, he has no full control of the winning percentage, because it also depends on the playing strength of the other teams in the league. So, we need to specify a relationship between the winning percentage and the number of talents.

In order to simplify the analysis, we will consider the case of a two-team league with a large-market team x and a small-market team y. This will also allow the main results to be presented graphically. The winning percentage of a team can then be specified by the simple contest success functions:

$$w_x = \frac{t_x}{t_x + t_y} \quad and \quad w_y = \frac{t_y}{t_x + t_y}. \tag{3.2}$$

Based on (3.2), the ratio of the winning percentages of the two teams is the same as the ratio of the talents: $\frac{w_x}{w_y} = \frac{t_x}{t_y}$.

The impact of an extra talent on a team's winning percentage is then equal to:

$$\frac{\partial w_x}{\partial t_x} = \frac{t_x + t_y - t_x\left(1 + \frac{\partial t_y}{\partial t_x}\right)}{(t_x + t_y)^2}. \tag{3.3}$$

In a competitive player market with a market clearing unit cost of talent, the sum of the talents of both teams in the denominator of (3.3) can be considered as the total supply of talent. If this supply of talent is fixed and, assuming perfect information, team owners are aware of the external effect that hiring one more talent implies an equal loss of talent in the other team, so the conjecture is $\frac{\partial t_y}{\partial t_x} = -1$. If they take this information into account when calculating the marginal revenue of talent, it follows that (3.3) simplifies to:

$$\frac{\partial w_x}{\partial t_x} = \frac{1}{(t_x + t_y)} = \frac{1}{s} = 1 \quad and\ thus\ also \quad \frac{\partial R_x}{\partial t_x} = \frac{\partial R_x}{\partial w_x}, \tag{3.4}$$

where s is the fixed talent supply. Because s is constant, it can be normalised to equal one, so the marginal revenue of talent is equal to the marginal revenue of winning. It follows that, by internalising the external effect of a constant talent supply, the winning percentage in revenue function (3.1) can simply be replaced by the number of talents.

However, by this substitution, the demand for talent of one team is not affected by the hiring strategies of the other team in the league, so a club owner has full control of the season winning percentage of his team (see Quirk and Fort, 1992; Vrooman, 1995). Under these assumptions, each profit-maximising team determines its downward-sloping demand curve for talent by comparing the marginal revenue and marginal cost of talent. The sum of both clubs' demand curves yields the market demand curve for talent and, together with the constant market supply curve, the market mechanism fixes the equilibrium unit cost of talent. This is the well-known Walras equilibrium model applied to the player labour market.

This approach has been criticised by Szymanski and Késenne (2004). They argued that the internalisation of the fixed talent supply is questionable. In the rat race for the best players, it seems reasonable to assume that, with a relatively limited number of teams in a league, clubs will react to the hiring strategies of their opponents in the league. So a game-theoretic approach is more appropriate, and a Nash equilibrium model, rather than a Walras equilibrium model, should be used to analyse the player labour market.

Taking things step by step, we will first analyse the player labour market using the fixed-supply Walras equilibrium model in section 3.3. Section 3.4 presents the Nash equilibrium model with a flexible talent supply.

3.3   Walras equilibrium

As discussed above, if the supply of talent is fixed and if the external effect is internalised in the hiring decisions of all club owners, the winning percentage in revenue function (3.1) can simply be replaced by the number of talents. Because one of the conditions was that the total talent supply in (3.4) is normalised to equal one, this implies that not only the sum of the winning percentages but also the sum of talents equals unity.

Leaving out the fixed ticket price, the revenue function of each team, based on the assumptions on the impact of market size and playing talent in (2.7), can now be simplified to:

$$R_x = R_x[m_x, t_x] \quad \frac{\partial R_x}{\partial m_x} > 0 \quad \frac{\partial R_x}{\partial t_x} > 0 \quad \frac{\partial^2 R_x}{\partial t_x^2} < 0 \quad \frac{\partial^2 R_x}{\partial t_x \partial m_x} > 0.$$

(3.5)

Each team's cost function is still $C_i = ct_i + c_i^0$ for $i: x, y$.

Obviously, the same conditions hold for team y.

With these general properties of the revenue and cost functions, the competitive market outcome in a profit- and a win-maximisation league will be analysed.

3.3.1 Profit maximisation

In a competitive player market where all clubs are profit maximisers, the market equilibrium can be found where the marginal revenue of talent of each club is equal to the marginal cost, which is equilibrium unit cost of talent c:

$$MR_x = \frac{\partial R_x[m_x, t_x]}{\partial t_x} = c = MR_y = \frac{\partial R_y[m_y, t_y]}{\partial t_y}.$$

If no further assumptions are made regarding the specification of the revenue function beyond concavity, little can be derived regarding the distribution of talents among teams (see Fort and Quirk, 2004). In order to derive any plausible results, one should start from a revenue function that is more 'well behaved' for the sports industry.

A reasonable starting point is to assume that spectators not only prefer to see their home team win but also care about the uncertainty of outcome in a game or the competitive balance in a league.

So, club revenues can be considered to be determined by the product of the market size and a linear combination of winning percentage and uncertainty of outcome. The uncertainty of outcome can, in its most simple form, be specified as the product of the winning percentages of the two teams, because this product reaches its highest value when both winning percentages are equal to 0.5. So, the revenue function can be written as:

$$R_i = m_i[(1 - \beta)w_i + \beta w_i(1 - w_i)] \quad \text{for } i: x, y, \tag{3.6}$$

where β is a constant parameter indicating the weights of winning and uncertainty of outcome. If spectators don't care about the uncertainty of outcome, the value of β will be close to zero.

Rearranging the terms of (3.6), one can derive that:

$$R_i = m_i w_i - m_i \beta w_i^2 \quad \text{for } i: x, y. \tag{3.7}$$

This specification turns out to result in a fairly simple revenue function for both team x and team y that is quadratic in the winning percentage. If the marginal revenue of an extra win can be derived as: $\frac{\partial R_i}{\partial w_i} = m_i - 2m_i\beta w_i$, it is also reasonable to assume that the marginal revenue of a win is zero if the winning percentage approaches 100 per cent or unity, so: $m_i - 2m_i\beta = 0$ or $\beta = \frac{m_i}{2m_i} = 0.5$.

Revenue function (3.7) then becomes: $R_i = m_i w_i - 0.5m_i w_i^2$ for $i: x, y$.

Given that the supply of talent is constant and normalised to equal unity, $\frac{\partial w_i}{\partial t_i} = 1$, revenue function (3.7) can also be written in terms of the number of talents:

$$R_i = m_i t_i - 0.5\, m_i t_i^2. \tag{3.8}$$

The demand or talent can then be derived for both teams as:

$$MR_i = \frac{\partial R_i}{\partial t_i} = m_i - m_i t_i,$$

which is a simple decreasing linear function in the number of talents. From the equalisation of the marginal revenue and the marginal cost c:

$$m_i - m_i t_i = c,$$

we find that $t_i = \frac{m_i - c}{m_i} = 1 - \frac{c}{m_i}$ for $i: x, y$,

which shows that the demand for talent is a positive function of the market size and a negative function of the cost of talent.

The competitive balance in a two-team league at the market equilibrium can then be found as:

$$m_x(1 - t_x) = c = m_y(1 - t_y) \text{ or } \frac{t_x^\pi}{t_y^\pi} = \frac{m_x}{m_y} \text{ with}$$

$$t_x^\pi = \frac{m_x}{m_x + m_y} \quad t_y^\pi = \frac{m_y}{m_x + m_y}. \tag{3.9}$$

It does not come as a surprise that the talent ratio is determined by the ratio of the market sizes. The market clearing unit cost of talent can then be found by substituting t_x^π or t_y^π into the marginal revenue function, so $c^\pi = \frac{m_x m_y}{m_x + m_y}$. What this result shows is that the equilibrium unit cost of talent will be lower, the more the market sizes of the two competing clubs deviate, all else being

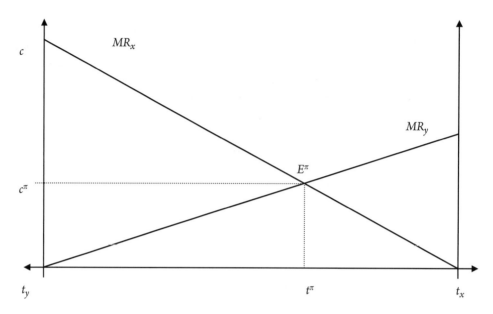

Figure 3.1 Profit maximisation

equal. The unit cost of talent will be at its highest level if the market sizes of the two teams are the same.

This market equilibrium is shown graphically in Figure 3.1, where the unit cost of talent is measured on the vertical axis, and the number of playing talents on the horizontal axis. The origin of the large-market club is on the left side of Figure 3.1; the origin of the small-market club is on the right side. The distance between the two origins indicates the constant supply of playing talent. Both clubs have a linear and downward-sloping demand curve (the marginal revenue curves MR_i). Because the market of team x is larger than the market of team y, the demand curve of team x starts at a higher level on the vertical axis. The slopes of the two demand curves are different, because they also depend on the market size. The player market equilibrium can then be found at point E^π, where the two demand curves intersect, because, at this point, the sum of the talent demands of both teams equals the constant talent supply.

The equilibrium salary level or unit cost of talent is c_π. If the salary level is higher than c_π, one can see in Figure 3.1 that total demand for talent would be lower than total supply of talent, and the flexible player salary would come down in a competitive market. If the salary level is lower than the equilibrium value, total demand would be higher than total supply and the player salary level would go up. In the equilibrium point, the distribution of playing talent between both clubs can be seen on the horizontal axis. Figure 3.1 shows that, at the market equilibrium, the large-market club has more talents than the small-market club (see also Quick and Fort, 1992).

3.3.2 Comparing profit and win maximisation

In Chapter 1, we mentioned that different club objectives can be expected to have a different impact on the number of talents hired by a team. In this section we will investigate what difference it makes in a Walras equilibrium model if both teams in a league are win maximisers. Given the specifications of the model, the only way team owners can maximise the team's winning percentage is by hiring as many talents as they can afford within the limits of their budget. So, the decision model can also be written as:

$$\max t_i \text{ subject to: } R_i[m_i, t_i] - ct_i - c_i^0 = \pi_i^0 \quad \text{for } i: x, y,$$

where π_i^0 is a fixed amount of season profits. To start with the simplest model, we assume that the capital cost is zero, $c_i^0 = 0$, and that club owners are not interested in making profits. So, the number of talents is maximised under the breakeven constraint $\pi_i^0 = 0$. It follows that a club spends all its revenue on talent. Under these hypotheses, and using the Lagrange function: $L_i = t_i + \lambda_i (R_i[m_i, t_i] - ct_i)$, the first-order conditions for win maximisation can then be written for both teams as:

$$\frac{\partial L_i}{\partial t_i} = 1 + \lambda_i \left(\frac{\partial R_i}{\partial t_i} - c \right) = 0$$
$$\quad \text{for } i: x, y,$$
$$\frac{\partial L_i}{\partial \lambda_i} = R_i - ct_i = 0$$

where λ_i is the positive Lagrange multiplier. From the first equation, it can be seen that $MR_i = c - 1/\lambda_i < c$, so that the marginal revenue of talent is lower than the marginal cost. It follows that the demand for talent, for a given unit cost of talent, is higher if a club is a win maximiser rather than a profit maximiser.

The second equation shows that a club's demand curve for talent is not given by the marginal revenue curve but by the average revenue curve, which is the revenue per unit of talent, or $\frac{R_i}{t_i} = AR_i = c$.

Remember that the average revenue increases if the marginal revenue is higher than the average revenue. If the marginal revenue is lower than the average revenue, the average revenue decreases. It follows that the marginal revenue curve runs through the maximum point of the average revenue curve. In the

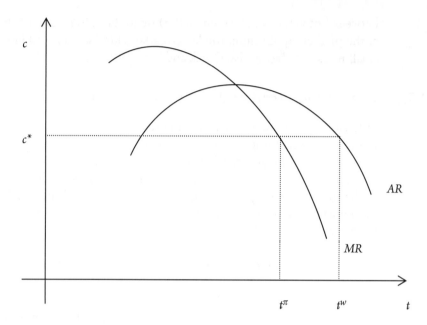

Figure 3.2 Marginal revenue (*MR*) and average revenue (*AR*)

relevant downward-sloping part of the average revenue curve, the marginal revenue curve is below the average revenue curve and also steeper than the average revenue curve. This is shown graphically in Figure 3.2. For a given salary level or unit cost, if talent c^*, a profit maximiser, is hiring t^π talents, a win maximiser is hiring t^w talents.

The demand for talent in a win-maximisation league can then be found by solving:

$$AR_i = \frac{R_i[m_i, t_i]}{t_i} = c \quad \text{for } i: x, y.$$

With the quadratic revenue function as specified above, the average revenue curve is also linear, but with a slope that is half the slope of the marginal revenue curve,

$$AR_i = m_i - 0.5m_i t_i \quad \text{for } i: x, y.$$

A first implication of win maximisation is a higher demand for talent, compared with profit maximisation. From $m_i - 0.5\,m_i t_i = c$, one can derive that:

$$t_i^w = 2\left(\frac{m_i - c}{m}\right) > t_i^\pi = \frac{m_i - c}{m_i}.$$

A second implication is that the distribution of talent among the two teams in a competitive market equilibrium is more unequal if the clubs' objective is to win rather than to make profits. The talents hired in the market equilibrium can now be calculated by equalising the AR curves of both teams:

$$m_x - 0.5m_x t_x = c = m_y - 0.5m_y t_y \text{ with } t_y = (1 - t_x).$$

After some rearrangements of the terms, this results in the following competitive balance:

$$t_x^w = \frac{2m_x - m_y}{m_x + m_y} \text{ and } t_y^w = \frac{2m_y - m_x}{m_x + m_y} \text{ so}$$

$$\frac{t_x^w}{t_y^w} = \frac{2m_x - m_y}{2m_y - m_x}. \tag{3.10}$$

Compared with a profit-maximisation league, the large-market team has more talents in a win-maximisation league, because $2m_x - m_y > m_x$, and the small-market team has fewer talents, because $2m_y - m_x < m_y$. Obviously, the distribution of talents, or the competitive balance, will be more unequal:

$$\frac{t_x^w}{t_y^w} = \frac{2m_x - m_y}{2m_y - m_x} > \frac{t_x^\pi}{t_y^\pi} = \frac{m_x}{m_y}.$$

A third implication is that, given the same talent supply, the equilibrium unit cost of talent, or the average salary level, will also be higher than in a profit-maximisation league. After substitution of t_x^w into the average revenue function, one finds that:

$$c^w = \frac{3m_x m_y}{2(m_x + m_y)} > c^\pi = \frac{m_x m_y}{m_x + m_y}.$$

It follows that players in a win-maximisation league are overpaid, that is, they are paid above the value of their marginal productivity.

A fourth implication is that, in a win-maximisation league, total league revenue is lower than in a profit-maximisation league. By moving away from the profit-maximisation equilibrium, the playing talents are no longer efficiently allocated over the two teams. In a win-maximisation league, some players are not playing in the team where their marginal revenue is at the highest level. The competitive balance in both scenarios can be seen in Figure 3.3, which shows the demand curves for talent under both the

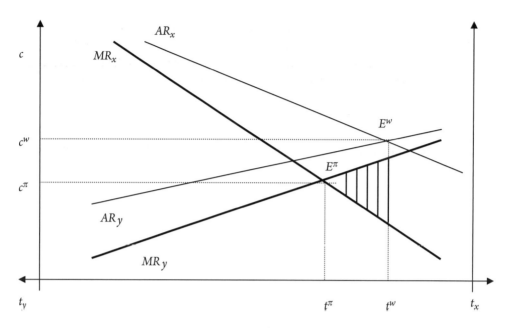

Figure 3.3 Win versus profit maximisation

profit- and the win-maximisation hypotheses. The point of intersection of the two MR curves yields the market equilibrium (E^π) in a profit-maximisation league, with a distribution of talent (t^π), and the market clearing unit cost of playing talent (c^π). The talent demand functions under win maximisation are given by the AR curves. The point of intersection of the AR curves indicates the market equilibrium in a win-maximisation league (E^w).

As can be seen, the distribution of talent in a win-maximisation league (t^w) is more unequal, and the unit cost of playing talent is higher $(c^w > c^\pi)$. Moreover, under win maximisation, all talents between the points t^π and t^w are playing in the large-market team, where their marginal revenue is lower than in the small-market team. This misallocation of talent in a win-maximisation league is causing a loss of total league revenue, which is indicated by the hatched area. By moving from E^π to E^w, the gain in revenue of the large-market team is offset by the loss in revenue of the small-market team. (See also Dietl, Lang and Werner, 2009 for the social welfare effects of profit and win maximisation.)

Remarks

1. Fort and Quirk (2004) have argued that nothing can be derived regarding the competitive balance in a win-maximisation league compared with

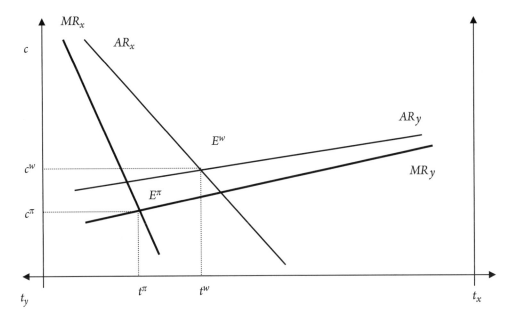

Figure 3.4 A rich club with a poor team

a profit-maximisation league if no simplifying assumptions are made for the revenue functions beyond concavity. However, as argued above, in order to be well behaved for sports, more assumptions are necessary for a team's revenue function. By assuming only that revenue functions are concave in talent, the very unlikely result can be found that, all else being equal, the small-market team hires more talents than the large-market team. In the two-club model with quadratic revenue functions, and with the slope of the demand curve of the large-market team much steeper than the slope of the demand curve of the small-market team, as shown in Figure 3.4, the small-market team hires more talents then the large-market team, and the distribution of talent is more equal in the win-maximisation league.

2. Dobson and Goddard (2001), starting from the well-known Cobb–Douglas specification of the revenue function, have shown that the distribution of talent is the same under profit and win maximisation. Indeed, for:

$$R_i = m_i^\alpha t_i^\beta \text{ for } i = x, y \text{ with } 0 < \alpha < 1 \text{ and } 0 < \beta < 1$$

one can derive that the competitive balance under profit and win maximisation is:

$$\frac{t_x}{t_y} = (m_x^\alpha/m_y^\alpha)^{\beta-1} > 1.$$

Does it mean that one of the conclusions above, that the competitive balance in a win-maximisation league is more unequal than in a profit-maximisation league, is not generally true? The fact is that one has to add at least one more assumption to the specification of the revenue function in order to make it well behaved for the sports industry. The diminishing effect of the winning percentage on the marginal revenue must be stronger the more a team's winning percentage approaches 100 per cent. This implies that the third-order partial derivative of the revenue function with respect to the winning percentage, or the number of talents, should be negative, or zero at the utmost, but certainly not positive as it is in the Cobb–Douglas function. In the graphical presentation of Figure 3.1, this means that the marginal revenue curves should be concave to the origin, or linear at best, but not convex as with the Cobb–Douglas specification.

3. We can relax the assumption of a zero capital cost and/or a zero profit rate. If the club's budget constraint is $R_i = ct_i + c_i^0 + \pi_i^0$, the demand curves for talent in a win-maximisation league are the net average revenue curves:

$$NAR_i = \frac{R_i - c_i^0 - \pi_i^0}{t_i}.$$

If we assume that the total capital compensation is more or less proportional to the club's revenue, $c_i^0 + \pi_i^0 = k_i R_i$, where k_i is the proportionality factor, the net average revenue curves become:

$$NAR_i = \frac{(1 - k_i)R_i}{t_i} = (1 - k_i)AR_i,$$

with $(1 - k_i)$ being the team's wage/turnover ratio. In the two-team model with quadratic revenue functions, the net average revenue curves are again linear, but less steep than the average revenue curves. This does not change the competitive balance in a win-maximisation league, if all teams have the same wage/turnover ratio, but it lowers the player salary level. This is shown in Figure 3.5. However, if the wage/turnover ratio is higher (lower) in the small-market club, the competitive balance will be more equal (unequal).

4. One can also consider the possibility that, in a league, one club is a profit maximiser while the other club is a win maximiser. If the large-market club is assumed to be more profit orientated and the small-market club is

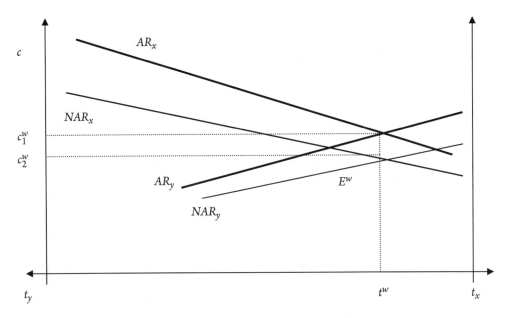

Figure 3.5 Average revenue (AR) and net average revenue (NAR)

more win orientated, the competitive balance in the league will be more equal. This can be seen in Figure 3.3, by considering the point of intersection of the marginal revenue curve of club x, being the profit maximiser, and the average revenue curve of club y, being the win maximiser.

5. John Vrooman (1995), in his well-known paper 'A General Theory of Professional Sports Leagues', started from more general revenue and cost functions, such as:

$$ R_i = R_0 m_i^\alpha w_i^\beta \qquad \text{and} \qquad C_i = C_0 m_i^\gamma w_i^\delta, $$

and derived that the competitive balance in a league can also be affected by differences in the revenue elasticity of winning. If the revenue elasticity of a win (β) is larger for a small-market team, the dominance of the large-market team can be reduced. The competitive balance will also improve if the cost elasticity of winning (δ) increases. The existence of negative cost externalities of market size (γ) can also improve the competitive balance.

6. As a last remark, we again consider club objective function (1.3), which was proposed by Rascher (1997), a linear combination of profits and wins (or talent):

$$\max \; (R_i - ct_i - c_i^0 + \alpha_i t_i) \quad \text{with} \quad \alpha_i > 0 \quad \text{for all } i.$$

The talent market equilibrium condition can then be written as:

$$MR_i + \alpha_i = c \quad \text{for } i\text{: } x, y.$$

It follows that, for a given unit cost of talent, the demand will be higher than under profit maximisation. Also, the more win orientated clubs are, that is, the larger the value of α_i, the higher the demand for talent will be. It follows that the equilibrium salary level will also be higher. The competitive balance in the two-team league can then be derived as:

$$\frac{t_x}{t_y} = \frac{m_x + \alpha_x - \alpha_y}{m_y + \alpha_y - \alpha_x}.$$

It follows that the competitive balance will be the same as under profit maximisation if the value of α_i is the same for both clubs, but differences in the motivation for winning affect the talent distribution. If the small-market clubs are more win orientated, the distribution of talents will be more balanced.

From this result, one can also derive that, depending on the α_i values, the small-market team can be more talented even if $m_x > m_y$. If the small-market club is much more win orientated than the large-market club, compared with the difference in market size, it is possible that the small-market team will dominate the large-market team.

3.3.3   Segmented player labour market

It is well known that some star players in professional team sports are among the best-paid workers in the world, making much more money than their grass-roots team mates. Some moderate professional players have to play at the minimum wage or are unemployed because they cannot find a team. The extremely high salaries of top athletes can be explained by Rosen's (1981) 'economics of super-stars', showing that small differences in performance can cause large differences in pay in a winner-takes-all competition. The classic example is that of an opera singer: because every opera lover wants to listen to the best tenor in the world, he will sell many more recordings than the second-best tenor. Sports teams also fight to hire the top players, and are prepared to pay them skyrocketing salaries, while the sub-top players have to settle for much less.

The model of the player labour market, in terms of the number of talents, cannot deal with this segmentation of the player labour market. In this section, we follow a somewhat different approach, where two types of players are considered, the top players and the regular players.

We start again from a well-behaved club revenue function in market size and winning percentage:

$$R_i = R_i[m_i, w_i] \quad \text{for all } i. \tag{3.11}$$

We call the number of top players l^T and the number of regular players l^R. The winning percentage of a club depends on the number of top players in the team. We assume that the productivity of a regular player, which is his individual contribution to a club's winning percentage, is only a fraction ε of the productivity of a top player. We can describe this relationship as:

$$w_i = l_i^T + \varepsilon l_i^R \quad \text{with } 0 < \varepsilon < 1. \tag{3.12}$$

Obviously, a team can have only a fixed number of players L on the field. So, a club faces the restriction that:

$$l_i^T + l_i^R = L \quad \text{for } i: x, y. \tag{3.13}$$

After the substitution of (3.12) and (3.13) in (3.11), the revenue function can be rewritten as:

$$R_i = R[m_i, \varepsilon L + (1 - \varepsilon)l_i^T]. \tag{3.14}$$

On the cost side, we assume that a club's total cost consists only of player salaries. If c^T is the cost or the salary of a top player and c^R is the cost of a regular player, we can write the cost function, given constraint (3.13), as:

$$C_i = (c^T - c^R)l_i^T + c^R L. \tag{3.15}$$

Because the regular players are in excess supply, we assume that their salary is simply equal to a fixed minimum wage. The salary of the top players, however, is determined by demand and supply on the market. We assume that the supply of top players L_s^T is constant.

The optimal number of top players of a profit-maximising club can now be found where the marginal revenue of top players equals the difference between their salary level and the (minimum) salary of the regular players:

$$MR_i^T = (1 - \varepsilon) \frac{\partial R_i}{\partial w_i} = c^T - c^R \quad \text{for } i: x, y.$$

So, the marginal revenue of top players also depends on the difference in player productivity $(1 - \varepsilon)$. Once the number of top players is determined, the number of regular players is given by $l_i^R = L - l_i^T$.

Considering again the two-team model, where x is the large-market club and y is the small-market club, the equilibrium on the labour market segment of top players is found where the marginal revenue of both clubs is equal to the salary difference:

$$MR_x^T = c^T - c^R = MR_y^T.$$

Because the market size has a positive effect on the marginal revenue of top players, it follows that the large-market club will hire more top players than the small-market club.

This result can also be seen in Figure 3.6, where the demand curves for top players of the large and the small club intersect at point E. The distribution of top players between the two teams is indicated on the horizontal axis and the salary difference between top and regular players on the vertical axis. The

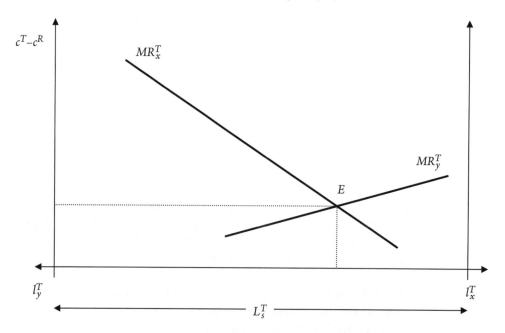

Figure 3.6 Top players' market equilibrium in a profit-maximisation league

model also shows that the salary difference between the star players and the grass-roots players can be very large if there is a limited supply of top players.

Because the revenue and cost functions (3.14) and (3.15) are in terms of the number of top players only, this model is very similar to the model in terms of playing talents, analysed in the previous sections. So, everything that has been derived from the model of the player market in terms of talents can also be interpreted as a model in terms of top players, where the unit cost of talent can be interpreted as the difference between the top player salary and the fixed minimum salary of the regular players.

3.4 Nash equilibrium

The Walras equilibrium model in section 3.3 cannot be used if the supply of talent is flexible. In the national football leagues in Europe, certainly after the liberalisation of the player labour market by the Bosman verdict of the European Court of Justice (1995), clubs hire talents from other national leagues, even in the middle of a season. It follows that an extra talent in one club does not necessarily imply a loss of talent in another club in the same league. But, even if the supply of talent is fixed, one can argue that a Nash equilibrium model rather than a Walras equilibrium model applies. If the talent supply is fixed, strengthening a team by hiring one more talent has a negative external effect on another team that loses a talent. In the Walras model, we have assumed that a club takes this externality into account in calculating its marginal revenue, so that the externality is internalised. In a competitive market, with perfect information, club owners, in their decisions on talent demand, are assumed to use all the information available. Under these conditions, as discussed in the previous sections, the winning percentage in the revenue function could simply be replaced by the number of playing talents, and the hiring strategy of a club would not be affected by the strategies of other clubs. Szymanski (2004) and Szymanski and Késenne (2004), however, argue that it is more appropriate, given the relatively limited number of teams in a league, to use a game-theoretic approach, because team owners, in their rat race for the best players, will react to the hiring strategies of their opponents. The internalisation of the external effects should be questionable, because, given the adding-up condition, it leaves one team without a choice of strategy.

Starting again from the two clubs' season revenue function $R_i[m_i, w_i]$ with:

$$\frac{\partial R_i}{\partial m_i} > 0 \quad \frac{\partial R_i}{\partial w_i} > 0 \quad \frac{\partial^2 R_i}{\partial w_i^2} < 0 \quad \frac{\partial^2 R_i}{\partial w_i \partial m_i} > 0 \quad \text{for } i: x, y$$

and

$$w_x = \frac{t_x}{t_x + t_y} \quad and \quad w_y = \frac{t_y}{t_x + t_y},$$

the impact of talent on winning percentage can be derived as in equation (3.3), which is repeated here:

$$\frac{\partial w_x}{\partial t_x} = \frac{(t_x + t_y) - t_x\left(1 + \frac{\partial t_y}{\partial t_x}\right)}{(t_x + t_y)^2}.$$

If the supply of talent is flexible, a talent increase in one team does not lower the talents of the opponent team in the league, so we can no longer assume that $\frac{\partial t_y}{\partial t_x} = -1$ as before. Now, $\frac{\partial t_y}{\partial t_x} = 0$, so the effect of talent on winning is:

$$\frac{\partial w_x}{\partial t_x} = \frac{t_y}{(t_x + t_y)^2} \quad and \quad \frac{\partial w_y}{\partial t_y} = \frac{t_x}{(t_x + t_y)^2}. \tag{3.16}$$

It follows that, when deriving the marginal revenue of talent, the hiring of talent of team x also depends on the hiring strategy of team y, and a game-theoretic approach is called for. Instead of the Walras equilibrium model, a non-cooperative Nash equilibrium model applies.

In sections 3.4.1 and 3.4.2, we will discuss the Nash equilibrium under both the profit- and the win-maximisation hypotheses. In section 3.4.3, the non-internalised fixed-supply model is investigated. Regarding the unit cost of talent, the usual assumption in a Nash equilibrium approach is that it is the reservation wage which is exogenously given, implying that the supply of talent is infinitely elastic. In the non-internalised fixed-supply model, however, it is possible that all teams are wage takers in an internationally competitive player market, and that the player cost is determined by international demand and supply conditions. Another possibility is that salaries are determined by collective bargaining agreements between team owners and players. As is often the case in the US major leagues, players can be united in a player association to counter the monopsony power of teams (see Chapter 5). In this case, the player labour market can be characterised as a bilateral monopoly. As most disputes are on salary levels and profits, the relative bargaining power of players and owners, threatening with player strikes and owner lockouts, will fix the salary level or, as in most cases, the league's salary cap (see Chapter 7). Other possibilities are that team owners pay a win bonus to the players, or unilaterally fix efficiency wages. The latter two cases will be discussed in sections 3.4.4 and 3.4.5.

3.4.1 Profit maximisation

We start again from the two-team model with quadratic revenue functions:

$$R_x = m_x w_x - 0.5 m_x w_x^2$$

$$R_y = m_y w_y - 0.5 m_y w_y^2 \quad \text{with} \quad m_x > m_y.$$

With an exogenous marginal cost of talent c, and assuming profit maximisation, the following reaction functions can be derived for the non-cooperative Nash equilibrium:

$$\frac{\partial R_x}{\partial w_x} \frac{\partial w_x}{\partial t_x} = (m_x - m_x w_x) \frac{t_y}{(t_x + t_y)^2} = c$$

$$\frac{\partial R_y}{\partial w_y} \frac{\partial w_y}{\partial t_y} = (m_y - m_y w_y) \frac{t_x}{(t_x + t_y)^2} = c. \tag{3.17}$$

These reaction functions can be simplified as follows:

$$(m_x - m_x w_x) w_y = c(t_x + t_y) \qquad m_x(1 - w_x) w_y = c(t_x + t_y)$$

$$(m_y - m_y w_y) w_x = c(t_x + t_y) \quad \text{or} \quad m_y(1 - w_y) w_x = c(t_x + t_y).$$

Equalising the two left-hand sides of the equations, $m_x w_y^2 = m_y w_x^2$, yields the following competitive balance:

$$\frac{w_x^\pi}{w_y^\pi} = \sqrt{\frac{m_x}{m_y}} \quad \text{with} \quad w_x^\pi = \frac{\sqrt{m_x}}{\sqrt{m_x} + \sqrt{m_y}} \quad \text{and}$$

$$w_y^\pi = \frac{\sqrt{m_y}}{\sqrt{m_x} + \sqrt{m_y}},$$

or the ratio of the winning percentages is equal to the square root of the ratio of the market sizes. It can be seen that, compared with the Walras equilibrium in section 3.3.1, the competitive balance is more equal in the Nash equilibrium:

$$\sqrt{\frac{m_x}{m_y}} < \frac{m_x}{m_y}.$$

The intuitive explanation is that, in the fixed-supply Walras model, a team owner takes into account the external effect that hiring one more talent reduces the talents of the other team, which results in a higher marginal

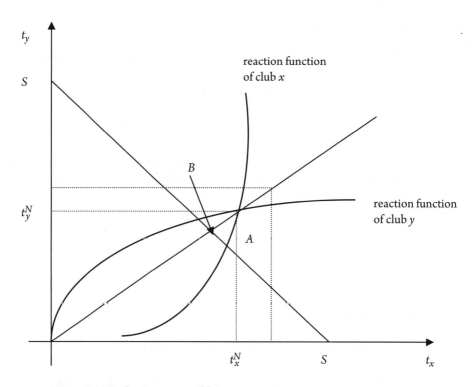

Figure 3.7 Nash–Cournot equilibrium

revenue of talent. So, a higher demand for talent will emerge, as well as a higher unit cost of talent. Furthermore, the negative external effect on the large-market team when the small-market team hires one more talent is larger than the negative external effect on the small-market team when the large-market team hires one more talent. As a consequence, the large-market team is better off in the Walras equilibrium where these external effects are internalised, that is, taken into account.

This Nash–Cournot model is presented graphically in Figure 3.7. On the vertical axis, the talents hired by club x are indicated, on the vertical axis the talents of club y. The Nash–Cournot equilibrium is found at the point of intersection A of the two non-linear reaction functions. The competitive balance or the distribution of talents is given by the slope of the line through the origin and equilibrium point A.

It is important to notice that the Nash equilibrium is inefficient, that is, total league revenue is not maximised. In general terms, the Nash equilibrium can be written as:

$$\frac{\partial R_x}{\partial w_x}\frac{\partial w_x}{\partial t_x} = \frac{\partial R_y}{\partial w_y}\frac{\partial w_y}{\partial t_y} \quad \text{with} \quad \frac{\partial w_x}{\partial t_x} = \frac{t_y}{(t_x + t_y)^2} \quad \text{and} \quad \frac{\partial w_y}{\partial t_y} = \frac{t_x}{(t_x + t_y)^2}$$

or:

$$\frac{\dfrac{\partial R_x}{\partial w_x}}{\dfrac{\partial R_y}{\partial w_y}} = \frac{\dfrac{\partial w_y}{\partial t_y}}{\dfrac{\partial w_x}{\partial t_x}} = \frac{t_x}{t_y}.$$

It follows that, if $t_x > t_y$, the marginal revenue of winning is higher in the large-market team than in the small-market team. In order to reach equality between the marginal revenues of winning, which is the condition for maximum league revenue, the winning percentage of the stronger team has to go up, because club revenue is concave in the winning percentage, so total league revenue can be increased by moving talent from the weaker team to the stronger team. In other words, the equilibrium distribution of talent is not unbalanced enough to reach maximum league revenue (see Szymanski and Leach, 2005).

In this flexible-supply approach, clubs in one league can hire talents from another league. If the absolute quality of the league depends on the number of talents playing in the league ($s = t_x + t_y$), the absolute quality can vary. If the absolute quality is also assumed to affect club revenue, the following revenue function can be considered, where absolute quality is measured by the total supply of talent s:

$$R_i = m_i w_i - 0.5 m_i w_i^2 + \varepsilon_i s \quad \text{for all } i = x, y \quad \text{with } \varepsilon_x > \varepsilon_y.$$

Solving the reaction equations, and assuming that the effect of absolute quality on revenue is larger in the large-market club than in the small-market club, one can derive that:

$$m_x w_y^2 - m_y w_x^2 = (\varepsilon_y - \varepsilon_x)(t_x + t_y) < 0 \quad \text{and} \quad m_x w_y^2 < m_y w_x^2.$$

So: $\dfrac{w_x^\pi}{w_y^\pi} > \sqrt{\dfrac{m_x}{m_y}}.$

The competitive balance turns out to be more unequal than in the model without absolute quality affecting team revenue.

3.4.2 Win maximisation

For a win-maximising club under the breakeven condition, one can derive from the Lagrange function $L_i = w_i + \lambda_i(R_i - ct_i - c_i^0)$ that the first-order conditions are:

$$\frac{\partial L_i}{\partial t_i} = \frac{\partial w_i}{\partial t_i} + \lambda_i \frac{\partial R_i}{\partial w_i}\frac{\partial w_i}{\partial t_i} - \lambda_i c = 0$$

$$\frac{\partial L_i}{\partial \lambda_i} = R_i - ct_i - c_i^0 = 0 \quad \text{or}$$

$$\frac{\partial R_i}{\partial w_i} = c_i / \frac{\partial w_i}{\partial t_i} - \frac{1}{\lambda_i}$$

$$R_i = ct_i + c_i^0 \quad \text{for } i: x, y.$$

Because the Lagrange multiplier λ_i is positive, the marginal cost of a win, $c/\frac{\partial w_i}{\partial t_i}$, is now larger than the marginal revenue of a win, as distinct from the profit-maximisation model where $MR = MC$. From the second equation, which is the breakeven condition, it can also be derived that the demand for talent is given by the net average revenue, so that the reaction functions, with an exogenously given unit cost of talent, can be written as:

$$\frac{R_i - c_i^0}{t_i} = c \quad \text{for } i: x, y.$$

For a two-club model with quadratic revenue functions, assuming for simplicity that the compensation of capital (c_i^0) is zero, the two reaction functions can be written as:

$$\frac{m_x}{t_x + t_y} - 0.5m_x\frac{t_x}{(t_x + t_y)^2} = c = \frac{m_y}{t_x + t_y} - 0.5m_y\frac{t_y}{(t_x + t_y)^2}.$$

Solving this system of equations simplifies to:

$$m_x - 0.5m_x w_x = c(t_x + t_y) = m_y - 0.5m_y w_y.$$

So, with $w_y = 1 - w_x$ the Nash equilibrium yields the following competitive balance:

$$\frac{w_x^w}{w_y^w} = \frac{2m_x - m_y}{2m_y - m_x}.$$

It does not come as a surprise that the competitive balance, or the distribution of talent, is the same in the Nash equilibrium as in the Walras equilibrium in (3.10). If a team wants to win as much as possible within the limits of its budget, it will spend all its money on talent regardless of the hiring strategy of the other teams in the league. So again, the competitive balance is more unequal under win maximisation than under profit maximisation.

Dietl et al. (2011) investigated the competitive balance in a sports league with utility-maximising teams, using Rascher's (1997) specification of the utility function, which is a linear combination of profits and wins. However, as distinct from Rascher's fixed-supply model with Walrasian fixed-supply conjectures, they started from a two-team model with Nash conjectures. Not surprisingly, the win percentage of a team increases if it becomes more win orientated. The authors also analysed the effect of utility maximisation on club profits, as well as the impact of revenue sharing on competitive balance. One of the most interesting conclusions of their analysis was that revenue sharing under utility maximisation can increase the investment in talent, based on what they called the 'sharpening effect' of revenue sharing, as contrasted with the so-called dulling effect of revenue sharing on talent investment under profit maximisation.

3.4.3 Fixed talent supply and Nash conjectures (*)

If the talent supply is fixed and normalised to equal one, but not internalised, equation (3.16) can be simplified as:

$$\frac{\partial w_x}{\partial t_x} = t_y \text{ and thus also } \frac{\partial R_x}{\partial t_x} = \frac{\partial R_x}{\partial w_x} t_y. \tag{3.18}$$

It follows that the impact of talent on winning is no longer a constant, so in the revenue function the winning percentage can no longer be replaced by the number of talents.

In order to see the implications of this assumption, we consider again a two-team model with quadratic revenue functions. Using (3.18), the following non-linear demand equations for **profit-maximising** teams can be found:

$$\frac{\partial R_x}{\partial t_x} = (m_x - m_x w_x) \frac{t_y}{(t_x + t_y)^2} = c \qquad t_y = \sqrt{\frac{c}{m_x}}$$

$$\frac{\partial R_y}{\partial t_y} = (m_y - m_y w_y) \frac{t_x}{(t_x + t_y)^2} = c \quad \text{or} \quad t_x = \sqrt{\frac{c}{m_y}}. \tag{3.19}$$

From (3.19), the competitive market equilibrium can now be derived by equalising the two reaction functions, or by simply taking the ratio t_x/t_y, which yields the following competitive balance:

$$\frac{w_x^\pi}{w_y^\pi} = \sqrt{\frac{m_x}{m_y}}. \tag{3.20}$$

The competitive balance is the same as in the flexible-supply model. Comparing this result with the fixed-supply Walras equilibrium, one can conclude that the distribution of talent is more equal in the fixed-supply Nash equilibrium. The explanation is again to be found in the negative external effects that clubs have on each other when hiring new talent. The negative external effect imposed by the small-market team on the large-market team is larger than the externality imposed by the large-market team on the small-market team. So, the small-market team is better off if these externalities are not internalised (see Szymanski, 2006).

Comparing (3.18) and (3.4), a team's demand for talent will be lower in the Nash equilibrium model, because, without internalising the negative external effect that hiring talents has in the opponent team, the marginal revenue of talent hiring will be lower. It follows also that the market clearing salary level will be lower if the constant supply of talent is not internalised.

The equilibrium salary level can be found by equalising market demand and market supply:

$$\sqrt{\frac{c}{m_y}} + \sqrt{\frac{c}{m_x}} = 1 \quad \text{so} \quad c^\pi = \frac{m_x m_y}{(m_x + m_y + 2\sqrt{m_x m_y})}.$$

This salary level is clearly lower than the salary level we found in the Walras model in section 3.3.1.

In Figure 3.8, the two fixed-supply models are presented and compared graphically.

Both the linear and the quadratic demand curves under the profit-maximisation hypothesis are drawn. If the fixed supply of talent is internalised, the linear demand curves intersect at point E^π. If the fixed supply of talent is not internalised, the demand curves are non-linear and the point of intersection indicates that the competition is more balanced and the salary level is lower. It follows that this equilibrium does not result in an efficient

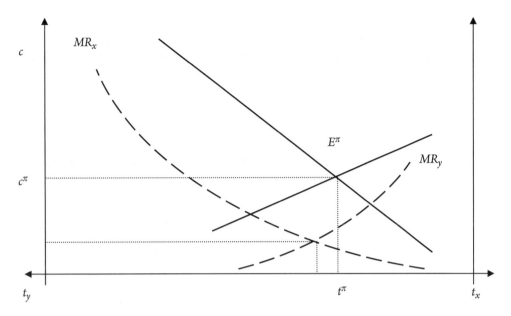

Figure 3.8 Comparing the fixed-supply models

allocation of talent, because not all available information was taken into account by the team owners.

In Figure 3.7, a constant supply of talent can be represented by a curve SS. Given the position of this curve, there is clearly an excess demand for talent in the initial equilibrium point A, so that, in a competitive player market, the unit cost of talent goes up and less talent is hired. The new equilibrium is found in point B at the point of intersection of the curve through the origin, representing the competitive balance, and the constant-supply curve SS, so that the competitive balance in point B is the same as in point A.

Given the results of the Nash equilibrium models for both the flexible- and the fixed-talent supply, the conclusion still stands that the competitive balance will be more unbalanced under win maximisation than under profit maximisation and that the market clearing salary level will be higher.

3.4.4 Win bonus (*)

In a sports league, team owners can expect to increase player performances, and the team's winning percentage or profits, by providing a win bonus to the team on top of the players' fixed salary level. In this section, we investigate what the impact of a win bonus is on the winning percentage, the competitive balance, the owner profits and the overall quality in a professional sports league. We extend the two-club model by introducing a simple premium system where a season win bonus is paid on top of a fixed player salary. We consider again profit maximisation and win maximisation. The impact of a premium system can be investigated by introducing a win bonus in just one club. This can also be interpreted as a more generous premium system in one club compared with the premium system in the other club.

If only the small-market club introduces a win bonus, the contest functions of both the large-market team x and the small-market team y can be written as:

$$w_x = \frac{t_x}{t_x + et_y} \qquad \frac{\partial w_x}{\partial t_x} = \frac{et_y}{(t_x + et_y)^2}$$

$$w_y = \frac{et_y}{t_x + et_y} \quad \text{so that} \quad \frac{\partial w_y}{\partial t_y} = \frac{et_x}{(t_x + et_y)^2},$$

where e is an index for effort or efficiency. If the effort players are willing to make depends on the win bonus σ, the effort function can be written as:

$$e = e[\sigma] \quad \text{with} \quad e[0] = 1 \quad e \geq 1 \quad e' > 0.$$

Notice that this also implies that the talent ratio is no longer equal to the ratio of the winning percentages:

$$\frac{w_x}{w_y} = \frac{t_x}{et_y}.$$

On the cost side, we assume that the player cost is the only cost of production. Because the large-market club does not introduce a bonus, its cost function is simply $C_x = ct_x$, where c is the exogenously given unit cost of talent. The small-market club's cost, however, consists of a fixed basic salary and a bonus depending on the team's winning percentage at the end of the season. However, it is most likely that the small-market club will decide to pay a lower fixed salary level to make up for the extra cost of the win bonus. If the small-market club pays a certain percentage θ of the fixed salary level c, its cost function can be written as:

$$C_y = \theta ct_y + \sigma w_y \quad 0 \leq \theta \leq 1 \quad 0 < \sigma < \frac{\partial R_y}{\partial w_y}.$$

It is important to mention here that there is a lot of uncertainty involved in this model. At the start of the season, when the decision on the size of the win bonus has to be made, club managers do not know what the response of the players and the team's winning percentage will be. They can only rely on an expected value of the effort to predict their season revenue and cost. Also, the managers cannot change the number of playing talents of the team during the season, because players are assumed to be under contract for at least one season.

If clubs are **profit maximisers**, the non-cooperative Nash–Cournot equilibrium, given a fixed unit cost of talent, can be found by solving the two reaction equations:

$$\frac{\partial R_x}{\partial w_x}\frac{\partial w_x}{\partial t_x} = c = \frac{1}{\theta}\frac{\partial w_y}{\partial t_y}\left(\frac{\partial R_y}{\partial w_y} - \sigma\right).$$

So

$$\frac{t_x^\pi}{t_y^\pi} = \frac{\dfrac{\partial w_y}{\partial t_y}}{\dfrac{\partial w_x}{\partial t_x}} = \frac{\theta\dfrac{\partial R_x}{\partial w_x}}{\dfrac{\partial R_y}{\partial w_y} - \sigma} \quad \text{and} \quad \frac{w_x^w}{w_y^w} = \frac{\theta\dfrac{\partial R_x}{\partial w_x}}{e\left(\dfrac{\partial R_y}{\partial w_y} - \sigma\right)}.$$

Because little can be derived from this general expression, we consider a simplified revenue function that is linear in the winning percentage, but concave in talent:

$$R_x = \alpha w_x \quad \text{and} \quad R_y = w_y \quad \text{with} \quad \alpha = \frac{m_x}{m_y} > 1.$$

For these revenue functions, it must hold that $0 < \sigma < 1$. The Nash–Cournot equilibrium for two profit-maximising teams, without the premium system, results in the following competitive balance or the talent ratio:

$$\frac{w_x^\pi}{w_y^\pi} = \frac{t_x^\pi}{t_y^\pi} = \alpha > 1.$$

If the premium system is introduced by the small-market team only, the reaction functions can be written as:

$$\frac{\alpha e t_y}{(t_x + et_y)^2} = c = \frac{e(1 - \sigma)t_x}{\theta(t_x + et_y)^2},$$

so the Nash–Cournot equilibrium yields the following talent and win ratio:

$$\frac{t_x^\pi}{t_y^\pi} = \alpha\frac{\theta}{1 - \sigma} \quad \text{and} \quad \frac{w_x^\pi}{w_y^\pi} = \alpha\frac{\theta}{e(1 - \sigma)}.$$

What can be derived from these solutions by comparing these outcomes with the equilibrium in the benchmark scenario without the premium system, that is, where $\theta = 1$, $\sigma = 0$ and $e = 1$, and the talent ratio is $\frac{t_x^\pi}{t_y^\pi} = \frac{w_x^\pi}{w_y^\pi} = \alpha$?

The new talent ratio does not depend on the effort players are willing to make, but the winning percentage of the small-market team, and therefore also the competitive balance, is positively affected by the response to the bonus.

If the fixed salary level is not reduced ($\theta = 1$), a higher win bonus can improve or worsen the competitive balance, depending on the effort function. A win bonus on top of the full salary level will increase the small-market club's total cost, but it can also increase the team's revenue if the response to the bonus is strong enough, that is, if $e > 1/(1 - \sigma)$.

If a positive value of the win bonus is combined with a lower fixed salary ($\theta < 1$), the impact depends on the relative values of the parameters. If $\theta < e(1 - \sigma)$, the competitive balance improves compared with the benchmark.

Since teams are profit maximisers, we want to know the impact of the premium system on profits. To calculate the teams' cost, we need the number of talents that are hired by each club:

$$t_x^\pi = \frac{\alpha^2 \theta \, e \, (1 - \sigma)}{c\{\alpha\theta + e(1 - \sigma)\}^2}$$

$$t_y^\pi = \frac{\alpha e \, (1 - \sigma)^2}{c\{\alpha\theta + e(1 - \sigma)\}^2},$$

so, although the talent ratio t_x/t_y is not affected, the number of talents of each club is affected by the team's effort. The team's profits can then be calculated as:

$$\pi_x = \frac{\alpha^3 \theta^2}{\{\alpha\theta + e\,(1 - \sigma)\}^2}$$

$$\pi_y = \frac{e^2 \, (1 - \sigma)^3}{\{\alpha\theta + e\,(1 - \sigma)\}^2}.$$

From these profit functions, it can be derived that a higher win bonus paid by the small-market club, all else being equal, will increase the profits of the large-market club ($\frac{\partial \pi_x}{\partial \sigma} > 0$) and that a higher fixed salary level paid by the small-market club will lower its profits ($\frac{\partial \pi_y}{\partial \theta} < 0$).

Table 3.1 Simulation results: profit maximisation

	$\theta = 1$ $\sigma = 0$ $e = 1$	$\theta = 1$ $\sigma = 0.1$ $e = 1.3$	$\theta = 1$ $\sigma = 0.1$ $e^r = 1$	$\theta = 0.85$ $\sigma = 0.1$ $e = 1.3$	$\theta = 0.85$ $\sigma = 0.1$ $e^r = 1$
w_y^π	0.33	0.37	0.31	0.41	0.36
t_x^π	44	47	47	48	48
t_y^π	22	21	21	26	26
Q	66	68	68	74	74
π_x	89	80	91	70	82
π_y	11	12	7	15	10
c_y	1	1.18	1.15	1	0.99

Because it is difficult to derive the combined impact of a change in two or more parameters, we look at a few results from a simple simulation exercise. In Table 3.1, calculations are made for different values of the fixed salary and the bonus parameter. We assume that the market of the big club is twice as large as the market of the small club ($\alpha = 2$). The exogenously given salary level is normalised to equal one ($c = 1$). The first column presents the benchmark case where no win bonus is paid.

In the second column, where the fixed salary is not reduced but a win bonus of 10 per cent is paid by the small-market club, which enhances the team's effort by 30 per cent, so that $e(1 - \sigma) > \theta = 1$, the winning percentage of the small-market club goes up. The small club hires fewer talents, but they are more efficient. The large club increases talent demand, and the total talents in the league, which can be seen as a measure of the absolute quality of the league (Q), are higher. Profits of the large club are down, but the small club's profits go up, because its revenue increases more than its player cost. The unit cost of talent in the small-market club (c_y), or the player's compensation, is 18 per cent higher than in the large-market club.

As mentioned before, the team managers can rely only on the expected value of the effort at the start of the season when the players are given a season contract. If the number of talents cannot be changed during the season, we look at the results when the team's effort is not enhanced by the win bonus. This is done in the third column. The parameters are the same as in the second column, but it is assumed now that there is no realised effort ($e^r = 1$). This obviously worsens the position of the small club considerably. Winning percentage and profits are down; only their non-motivated players are happy. It is the large-market club that profits from the premium system introduced by the small-market club.

In the fourth column, the fixed salary level is lowered by 15 per cent with the 10 per cent win bonus. If the bonus increases effort as expected, the competitive balance strongly improves. The quality of the league is also up, as well as the profits of the small-market club. The players' compensation stays more or less the same as the players' compensation in the large-market club.

However, if the win bonus turns out to be ineffective, we can see in the fifth column that the premium system still improves the competitive balance, but reduces the small-market club's profits compared with the benchmark case. The profits of the large-market club are not as far down as in the case where the bonus was effective. At the end of the season, the player compensation in the small-market club turns out to be lower than in the large-market club.

These results show that a profit-maximising club has the best chance of increasing its profits by introducing a premium system that consists of a win bonus combined with a lower fixed salary level. But there is a risk: the condition is that players are responsive to the bonus, as expected by the manager. If they are not, profits will be down. Another risk is that players will run off to another team if their total pay is too low compared with that of the opponent teams. If a win bonus is paid on top of the full salary level, the response to the bonus must be strong enough for the club to increase its profits.

In a **win-maximisation** league, the assumption is that all club owners try to maximise the team's season winning percentage under the breakeven constraint. In that case, the Nash–Cournot equilibrium can be found from:

$$\frac{R_x[m_x, w_x]}{t_x} = c = \frac{1}{\theta} \frac{R_y[m_y, w_y] - \sigma w_y}{t_y}.$$

Again, little can be derived from this general solution. We therefore now use the simplified quadratic revenue function $R_i = m_i w_i - w_i^2$. If the small-market club introduces a premium system, the Nash–Cournot equilibrium can be found from:

$$\frac{m_x w_x - w_x^2}{t_x} = \frac{1}{\theta} \frac{(m_y - \sigma) w_y - w_y^2}{t_y}.$$

Multiplying both sides of the equation by $(t_x + e t_y)$, one can derive that:

$$m_x - w_x = \frac{e}{\theta}(m_y - \sigma - w_y), \quad \text{so} \quad w_y^w = \frac{\theta(1 - m_x) - e(\sigma - m_y)}{e + \theta}.$$

Table 3.2 Simulation results: win maximisation

	$\theta = 1$ $\sigma = 0$ $e = 1$	$\theta = 1$ $\sigma = 0.1$ $e = 1.3$	$\theta = 1$ $\sigma = 0.1$ $e' = 1$	$\theta = 0.85$ $\sigma = 0.1$ $e = 1.3$	$\theta = 0.85$ $\sigma = 0.1$ $e' = 1$
w_y^w	0.25	0.36	0.20	0.45	0.30
$t_x^{w(*)}$	94	87	87	80	80
$t_y^{w(*)}$	31	37	37	50	50
Q	125	124	124	130	130
π_x	0	0	9	0	12
π_y	0	0	−13	0	−12
C_y	1.0	1.1	1.05	0.94	0.94

Note: [*] Notice that, without profits or losses, $t_x = R_x = C_x$ and that $t_y = \frac{R_y - \sigma w_y}{\theta}$.

A simulation can again reveal what is going on in this scenario. In Table 3.2, it is assumed that the large club's market size is $m_x = 2$ and the small club's market size $m_y = 1.5$. The exogenous unit cost of talent is again equal to one ($c = 1$). In the first column, the results of the scenario without the premium system are given.

In the second column, the small-market club pays a win bonus of 10 per cent on top of the full fixed salary, which enhances effort by 30 per cent. This improves the competitive balance, but the total league quality stays more or less the same owing to the reduction in talent demand by the large-market club. The players of the small club are better off, because their pay goes up by 10 per cent.

As can be seen in the third column, things change dramatically for the small-market club if the team's effort has not improved as expected. Its winning percentage goes down, which causes a financial loss. Only the players are still happy, with 5 per cent extra pay. The winner is clearly the large-market team, with a higher winning percentage and an unexpected profit.

In the fourth column, the fixed salary is reduced to 85 per cent of the large-market club's salary level with the same win bonus and effort as in column 2. This clearly helps the small-market club to reach its objective. The competitive balance improves, as well as the quality of the league. Only the players will not be very happy, because their total pay is 6 per cent lower than the salary paid by the large-market club. Hence, there is again a risk that players will want to leave the club at the end of the season.

If the players' effort does not react to the win bonus, the fifth column shows that the small-market team still reaches a higher winning percentage than without the premium system, but its increased win percentage has caused a financial loss. The club will also have to convince its players to stay, given their lower salary. As a win maximiser, the large-market club is not well off, although it realises an unexpected profit.

It is also possible that a financial loss will be made by the team that pays the bonus, because the response to the bonus is stronger than expected. This depends, among other things, on the specification of the revenue function. If the winning percentage has only a weak effect on season revenue, the season cost can be increased more than the season revenue, leading to a financial loss. If the actual effort is different from the expected effort, little can be concluded about the final impact of a premium system on profits and wins.

We can conclude that the impact of a premium system set up by a club in professional team sports is rather complex, given the fact that clubs also react to the strategies of other clubs in the league. The team that introduces a premium system, or a stronger premium system than its opponents, can expect to increase its profits or winning percentage by paying a win bonus combined with a reduced fixed salary. A crucial factor, though, is the players' response to the win bonus. If the team's effort is not enhanced enough by the bonus, the team's profits and winning percentage can go down. The effect that an increased winning percentage has on the current season revenue is also an important factor (see Késenne, 2006).

3.4.5 Efficiency wages (*)

Another hypothesis regarding wage determination is that salaries are unilaterally fixed by the owners. If one of the most important objectives of a team is playing success, team managers can be expected to pay higher salaries than the market salary in order to attract the better players (adverse selection model), or to prevent the good players from leaving the club (labour turnover model), or simply to stimulate players to perform. The winning percentage depends not only on the talents of the players, but also on the effort players are willing to make. So, it is worth investigating what the implications for the behaviour of teams are if the efficiency wage theory is introduced into the model (see Akerlof and Yellen, 1986).

Let us assume that the winning percentage is affected not only by the relative talent of a team but also by an index representing the effort the team is willing to make, where effort is a function of a club's salary level. Then, the winning percentage of team x can be written as:

$$w_x = f\left[e(c_x) \frac{t_x}{t_x + t_y} \right].$$

The effort function e is an increasing function of the club's salary level with decreasing marginal returns, that is, $e' > 0$ and $e'' < 0$, with primes indicating derivatives, and with f being a monotonously increasing function such that the adding-up condition $w_x + w_y = 1$ still holds. Most efficiency wage models introduce some kind of relative salary level in the effort functions. The argument goes that players are only willing to make an extra effort if their salary level is higher than the equilibrium salary level in a competitive player market, or higher than the salary paid in another club. This way, c_x can be interpreted as the level of the salary, relative to the market clearing salary level.

In this scenario, club managers have to decide on both the optimal talent level and the optimal salary level.

Under **profit maximisation**, the first-order partial derivatives of the profit function with respect to the salary level and the number of the playing talents have to equal zero:

$$\frac{\partial R_x}{\partial c_x} = \frac{\partial R_x}{\partial w_x} f' e' \frac{t_x}{t_x + t_y} = t_x \qquad (3.21)$$

$$\frac{\partial R_x}{\partial t_x} = \frac{\partial R_x}{\partial w_x} f' e \frac{t_y}{(t_x + t_y)^2} = c_x. \qquad (3.22)$$

Solving the first equation for $\frac{\partial R_x}{\partial w_x}$ and substituting it into the second equation, a variant of the so-called Solow condition (1979) can be derived, indicating that the wage elasticity of effort is:

$$\varepsilon_w = e' \frac{c_x}{e} = \frac{t_y}{t_x + t_y} < 1. \qquad (3.23)$$

From this solution one can derive that profit-maximising clubs are willing to pay higher efficiency wages than profit-maximising firms in other industries, for which Solow (1979) has derived that the effort elasticity $\varepsilon_i^\pi = 1$.

This can be illustrated in Figure 3.9, where the salary level is on the horizontal axis and effort on the vertical axis. The point of tangency between the

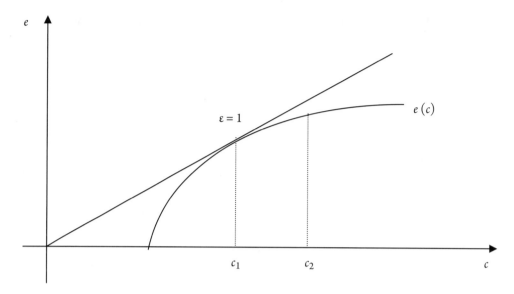

Figure 3.9 Effort function and efficiency wage

concave effort function and the slope of the line through the origin, indicating the ratio e/c, marks the point where the effort elasticity equals unity. To the right of this point, the effort elasticity is smaller than zero, so the optimal efficiency wage level is higher $(c_2 > c_1)$.

The efficiency wage model can explain why there is unemployment among professional players. One can expect that the optimal and rigid efficiency salary level in a club will be higher than the market clearing level. The excess supply of talent it causes will not seduce a team owner to lower the player salary level, because it will lower the efforts that his players are willing to make and therefore also the club's profits. Equation (3.23) also points out that a club's efficiency wage per unit of talent is set at a higher level the stronger the team is compared with its opponents in the league (see also Késenne, 2006).

? **EXERCISES 3**

3.1 In a constant-supply Walras equilibrium model with team revenue functions $R_x = 12t_x - 6t_x^2$ and $R_y = 8t_y - 4t_y^2$, and with the labour cost as the only cost, calculate the distribution of playing talent and the market clearing unit cost of talent under profit maximisation. Calculate also the revenues and the profits of the large- and the small-market club.

3.2 With the same revenue and cost functions as in exercise 3.1, what will be the distribution of playing talent and the market clearing unit cost of talent under win maximisation? Calculate the revenues of the large- and the small-market team. Compare with the profit-maximisation results of exercise 3.1.

3.3 Assume that the competitive balance in a profit maximisation league with only six teams is given by the following winning percentages w_i^p, which add up to 3:

0.70   0.65   0.55   0.50   0.35   0.25

What will be the corresponding winning percentages in a win-maximisation league?

3.4 With the same revenue and cost functions as in exercise 3.1, but with the large-market club as a profit maximiser and the small-market club as a win maximiser, what will be the distribution of playing talent and the equilibrium cost of talent?

3.5 With the same revenue and cost functions as in exercise 3.1, but starting from teams that want to maximise a linear combination of profits and wins, with weights $\alpha_x = 0$ and $\alpha_y = 4$, derive the distribution of talent and the unit cost of talent.

3.6 Given the following revenue functions in a two-team model under profit maximisation: $R_x = 12w_x - 6w_x^2$ and $R_x = 8w_x - 4w_x^2$, derive the competitive balance in a Nash equilibrium model with a constant supply of talent (=1). Also calculate the market clearing salary level.

Appendix

The *n*-club Walras model (*)

Starting from the season revenue function that is concave in the winning percentage:

$$R_i = R_i(m_i, w_i, p_i) \qquad \text{for } i: 1, n,$$

Borghans and Groot (2005) have derived the exact relationship between the season winning percentage and the talents of a team by starting from the winning probability of a team in an individual game:

$$w_{ij} = \frac{t_i}{t_i + t_j},$$

where t_i and t_j are the number of talents of the teams (not the number of players!), and w_{ij} is the probability that team i will win the game against team j. If there are n teams in the league and each team plays $n-1$ games, the expected number of wins is:

$$g_{wi} = \sum_{j \neq i}^{n} \frac{t_i}{t_i + t_j}.$$

The (expected) winning percentage is then:

$$w_i = \frac{g_{wi}}{n - 1} = \frac{1}{n - 1} \sum_{j \neq i}^{n} \frac{t_i}{t_i + t_j}. \tag{3A.1}$$

From this relationship one can derive that the sum of the winning percentages equals $n/2$. Although this relationship between winning percentage and talent is correct, it considerably complicates the derivation of the marginal revenue of talent. We therefore choose the following simple approximation of the winning percentage:

$$w_i = \frac{n}{2} \frac{t_i}{\sum_{j}^{n} t_j}. \tag{3A.2}$$

The winning percentage of a team is $n/2$ times the ratio of its talents to all talents in the league. Although the sum of these winning percentages is also equal to $n/2$, there is an important difference between the two measures. The ratio of the winning percentages of any two teams, based on (3A.2), is the same as the ratio of the talents: $\frac{w_i}{w_j} = \frac{t_i}{t_j}$, which is clearly not true for relationship (3A.1). Only in the special case of a two-team league are both expressions identical. Another disadvantage of this simplification is that the winning percentage of a team can be larger than one if that team holds more than $2/n$ per cent of total league talent.

Continuing with relationship (3A.2), the marginal impact of talent on the winning percentage can be calculated as:

$$\frac{\partial w_i}{\partial t_i} = \frac{n}{2} \frac{\sum\limits_{j=1}^{n} t_j - t_i\left(1 + \sum\limits_{j \neq i}^{n} \frac{\partial t_j}{\partial t_i}\right)}{\left(\sum\limits_{j=1}^{n} t_j\right)^2}. \tag{3A.3}$$

If the supply of talent is fixed and the external effects of talent hiring are internalised by club management, that is, if $\sum_{j \neq i}^{n} \left(\frac{\partial t_j}{\partial t_i}\right) = -1$, expression (3A.3) simplifies to: $\frac{\partial w_i}{\partial t_i} = \frac{n}{2s}$, where s is the constant talent supply $(s = \sum_{j=1}^{n} t_j)$. Because $n/2s$ is a constant, it can be normalised to equal one, so the marginal revenue of talent is equal to the marginal revenue of winning. It follows that, in the revenue function, the winning percentage can be replaced by the number of talents.

In this n-club model, we further simplify the quadratic revenue function by assuming that the slopes of the talent demand curves are the same in every team and equal to b:

$$R_i = m_i t_i - b t_i^2 \qquad \text{for all } i\text{: } 1, n.$$

The market equilibrium can now be found by putting the marginal revenues of all clubs equal to the market clearing unit cost of talent:

$$m_i - 2b t_i = c \qquad \text{for all } i\text{: } 1, n,$$

so that the demand for talent of each club can be written as:

$$t_i^\pi = \frac{m_i - c}{2b} \qquad \text{for all } i\text{: } 1, n. \tag{3A.4}$$

This result indicates that the size of the market increases the demand for talent and that the salary level reduces the demand. Given that the supply of talent is constant and equal to half the number of teams, $s = \sum_{i=1}^{n} t_i = \frac{n}{2}$, we can find the market clearing salary level in a competitive player market where market demand equals market supply:

$$\frac{\sum_{i=1}^{n} m_i - nc}{2b} = s = \frac{n}{2}, \qquad \text{so that} \qquad c^{\pi} = \overline{m} - \frac{2bs}{n} = \overline{m} - b.$$

From this solution one can see that the supply of talent has a positive effect, and the average market size, affecting the demand for talent, has a positive effect on the salary level. (In order to yield positive values for talent demand and salary level, it is necessary that $\overline{m} - m_i < b < \overline{m}$).

By substituting the salary level in expression (3A.4), the number of talents hired by all clubs can be found as:

$$t_i^{\pi} = \frac{1}{2} + \frac{m_i - \overline{m}}{2b} \qquad \text{for all } i: 1, n. \qquad (3A.5)$$

So, it is clear that the club with the largest market also has the largest number of talents. This market equilibrium, under perfectly competitive conditions, is Pareto optimal in the sense that all talents are efficiently allocated over the teams so that total league revenue is maximised.

Under **win maximisation**, the demand curves for talent are given by the average revenue, so:

$$m_i - bt_i = c \qquad \text{and} \qquad t_i^{w} = \frac{m_i - c}{b} \qquad \text{for all } i: 1, n.$$

The salary level can again be found by equalising the market demand for talent and the constant market supply of talent:

$$c^{w} = \frac{2\sum_{i=1}^{n} m_i - nb}{2n} = \overline{m} - \frac{b}{2}, \qquad \text{so that} \qquad c^{w} > c^{\pi}.$$

The distribution of talent among clubs is more unequal if the clubs' objective is to win rather than to make profits. The talents hired by the clubs can be calculated as:

$$t_i^{w} = \frac{1}{2} + \frac{m_i - \overline{m}}{b} \qquad \text{for all } i: 1, n, \qquad (3A.6)$$

so that the difference between the hiring of talents in both leagues is:

$$t_i^{w} - t_i^{\pi} = \frac{m_i - \overline{m}}{2b} \qquad \text{for all } i: 1, n.$$

A large-market club in a win-maximisation league has more talents than the same large-market club in a profit-maximisation league, and a small-market club in a win-maximisation league has fewer talents than the same small-market club in a profit-maximisation league. It follows that the competition is more unbalanced in a win-maximisation league than in a profit-maximisation league.

This can also be seen by substituting m_i from (3A.5) into (3A.6), so that it can be derived that:

$$t_i^w = 2t_i^\pi - 0.5 \qquad \text{for all i: } 1, n.$$

Using the standard deviation as an indicator of the talent distribution, it is clear that the standard deviation of t_i^w is twice the standard deviation of t_i^π.

4

Product and labour market

4.1 Introduction

In the previous chapters, when dealing with the ticket price, we kept the number of talents constant, and, when dealing with the demand for talent, the ticket price was fixed. In this chapter, we analyse ticket pricing, which was one of the important decisions of club owners in the product market, together with talent hiring, which was the most important decision in the labour market. We will investigate how ticket price and talent demand are connected and how this connection affects the decisions. If the number of talents of a team changes, it will affect its winning percentages and so the demand for tickets, with the result that the optimal ticket price is also affected. A change in the ticket price will change attendances and gate receipts, as well as other revenues, so the demand for talent is also affected. We therefore develop a two-decision variable model, where club owners have to fix simultaneously, at the start of the season, ticket price and talent demand. We will again compare the solutions under both the profit- and the win-maximisation hypotheses.

4.2 Ticket pricing and talent hiring

In this model, most hypotheses made in the previous chapters still hold: clubs are local monopolists and price makers on the product market, and wage takers on the player labour market. The unit cost of a playing talent is determined by demand and supply on a competitive player labour market. The supply of talent is fixed, and the marginal cost of spectators is zero. Initially, we assume that there are no stadium capacity constraints. Using the Walras equilibrium approach, the season winning percentage in the team's demand and revenue function for tickets can be replaced by the number of talents of the team:

$$A[m, t, p].$$

The usual assumptions, with subscripts indicating partial derivatives, hold:

$$A_m > 0 \quad A_p < 0 \quad A_t > 0 \quad A_{tt} = \frac{\partial^2 A}{\partial t^2} < 0. \tag{4.1}$$

However, a few more assumptions are added:

$$A_{tm} = \frac{\partial^2 A}{\partial t \partial m} > 0 \quad A_{pm} = \frac{\partial^2 A}{\partial p \partial m} > 0 \quad A_{pt} = \frac{\partial^2 A}{\partial p \partial t} = 0. \tag{4.2}$$

The first two inequalities state that the impacts of talent and ticket price on attendances are larger for large-market teams, which is a reasonable assumption. The sign of the last effect is less obvious. Because there seems to be no clear indication for this derivative to be large in a positive or negative sense, we simply assume it to be zero, which means that the demand function is strongly separable in ticket price and talent.

We assume again that all non-gate revenues are proportional to the number of attendances, with proportionality factor κ, so the club revenue function can be written as:

$$R = (p + \kappa)A[m, t, p].$$

Also, the club's season cost function is the same as before, consisting of labour and non-labour costs. The capital cost is constant in the short run and, in a competitive player market, the unit cost of a playing talent is the same for all clubs:

$$C = ct + c^0.$$

4.2.1 Profit maximisation

For a profit-maximising team, the first-order conditions are:

$$\pi_p = (p + \kappa)A_p + A = 0 \tag{4.3}$$

$$\pi_t = (p + \kappa)A_t - c = 0. \tag{4.4}$$

The first equation is the well-known pricing rule, showing that the price elasticity is smaller than one. The second equation indicates that talents are hired until marginal revenue equals marginal cost. The second-order conditions for a maximum require the Hessian matrix to be negative definite, so the following inequalities must hold:

$$\pi_{pp} < 0 \quad \pi_{tt} < 0 \quad \pi_{tt}\pi_{pp} - \pi_{pt}^2 > 0, \tag{4.5}$$

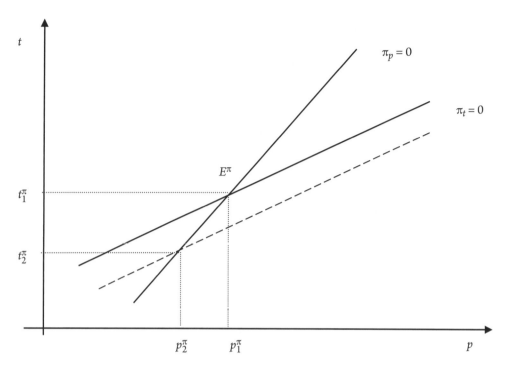

Figure 4.1 Profit-maximising equilibrium

where:

$$\pi_{tt} = (p + \kappa)A_{tt} < 0$$

$$\pi_{pp} = (p + \kappa)A_{pp} + 2A_p < 0$$

$$\pi_{pt} = \pi_{tp} = (p + \kappa)A_{pt} + A_t = A_t > 0.$$

These conditions can also be illustrated graphically. In Figure 4.1, the two decision variables are found on the axes.

From the total differential of the first-order conditions (4.3) and (4.4):

$$d\pi_p = \pi_{pp}dp + \pi_{pt}dt = 0$$

$$d\pi_t = \pi_{tp}dp + \pi_{tt}dt = 0.$$

The slopes of the locus $\pi_p = 0$ and the locus $\pi_t = 0$ in the p–t diagram can be derived to be:

$$\frac{dt}{dp}\bigg|_{\pi_p=0} = -\frac{\pi_{pp}}{\pi_{pt}} > 0$$

$$\frac{dt}{dp}\bigg|_{\pi_t=0} = -\frac{\pi_{pt}}{\pi_{tt}} > 0.$$

Given the properties of the demand function and the second-order conditions, both slopes are clearly positive. From the second-order conditions (4.5), we can also derive that the slope of the locus $\pi_p = 0$ is steeper than the slope of the locus $\pi_t = 0$. The first-order conditions for profit maximisation are met at the point of intersection E^π of the two loci, which marks the optimal price level p_1^π and the optimal number of playing talents t_1^π.

An interesting question is how a rise in player salary affects the optimal ticket price in a two-decision variable model. Remember that we found in Chapter 2 that the optimal ticket price was not affected by the player cost. But, in that one-decision variable model, the hiring of talent was kept constant. In this two-decision variable model, a club owner has to decide on the hiring of talent as well. From Figure 4.1, we can derive that a higher unit cost of talent will shift the locus $\pi_t = 0$ down, because, for a given price level, talent demand will come down with a higher salary level. It follows that in the new point of intersection the optimal ticket price p_2^π and talent demand t_2^π are lower. This result can also be derived algebraically. To derive the impact of an exogenous variable on both decision variables, we have to differentiate the first-order conditions (4.3) and (4.4) with respect to the exogenous unit cost of talent c, and solve for $\frac{\partial p}{\partial c}$ and $\frac{\partial t}{\partial c}$:

$$\frac{\partial p}{\partial c} = -\frac{\pi_{pt}}{\pi_{tt}\pi_{pp} - \pi_{pt}^2} < 0 \qquad \frac{\partial t}{\partial c} = \frac{\pi_{pp}}{\pi_{tt}\pi_{pp} - \pi_{pt}^2} < 0.$$

So, contrary to what is generally claimed by many club owners, who argue that player salaries have to be kept low in order to keep ticket prices low, a lower salary level turns out to increase the optimal ticket price set by a profit-maximising owner. Although somewhat counter-intuitive, this result can be explained by the fact that a lower salary increases the hiring of talent and the winning percentage, which causes the demand curve for tickets to shift to the right, so the profit-maximising ticket price will be set at a higher level.

Applying the envelope theorem to the profit function, $\frac{\partial \pi}{\partial c} = -t < 0$, it follows that lower player salaries increase owner profits, which is probably the real reason why club owners talk player salaries down.

Comparative static analysis also confirms that large-market clubs hire more talents and charge higher ticket prices than small-market clubs (see Demmert, 1973). In Figure 4.1, a larger value of m would shift the locus $\pi_t = 0$ upward (for a given price, a larger market will increase talent) and the locus $\pi_p = 0$ to the right (for given talent, a larger market will increase the ticket price), so, at the new point of intersection, both the ticket price and the demand for talent are higher.

4.2.2 Win maximisation

How does a **win-maximising club** set both ticket price and talent demand at the start of the season? If it is the club's objective to maximise the season winning percentage, it hires as many talents as the budget permits.

If the club maximises the number of playing talents under the breakeven constraint, the first-order conditions for win maximisation, as derived from the Lagrange function, are:

$$(p + \kappa)A_p + A = 0 \quad (p + \kappa)A_t = c - \frac{1}{\lambda}$$

$$(p + \kappa)A - ct - c^0 = 0,$$

where λ is the positive Lagrange multiplier. The first equation is the pricing rule, which turns out to be exactly the same as under profit maximisation. From the second equation it can be seen that a win-maximising club will hire playing talent up to a point where marginal revenue is lower than marginal cost. The third equation is the budget constraint.

What will the optimal ticket price and talent demand be compared with a profit-maximising club? One way to find out is to look at the iso-profit contours in the p–t diagram. If, in Figure 4.2, E^π is the profit-maximising point, it follows that turning away from this point in either direction means that profits decrease. The iso-profit contours are now ovals drawn round this point, such that all points on one oval indicate the same profit level. The further away these contours are from E^π, the lower the profits are. These contours can be found by putting the total differential of the profit function equal to zero:

$$d\pi = \pi_p dp + \pi_t dt = 0.$$

So, the slopes of the iso-profit contours are:

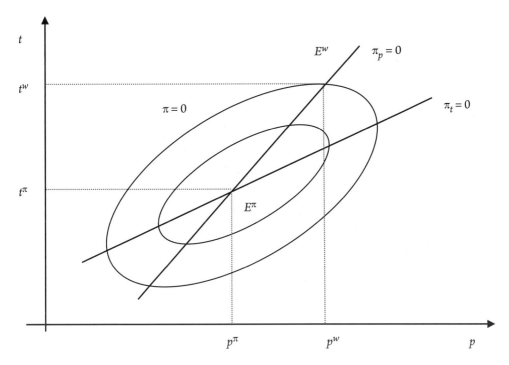

Figure 4.2 Win-maximising equilibrium

$$\left.\frac{dt}{dp}\right|_{d\pi=0} = -\frac{\pi_p}{\pi_t}.$$

It follows that the slopes are zero for all points (p, t) where $\pi_p = 0$, and infinite for all points (p, t) where $\pi_t = 0$.

These iso-profit contours can now be added to the graphical presentation of the first-order conditions in Figure 4.2. The wider these iso-profit contours, the further away they are from the profit-maximising point, and the lower the profits are. One of these contours is the zero-profit contour. If a club maximises the number of talents on the vertical axis, under the breakeven constraint, the equilibrium point is E^w with price p^w and playing talent t^w. It follows that both the demand for playing talent and the ticket price are higher in a win-maximising team than in a profit-maximising team.

Madden's (2012) objective of fan utility maximisation, or attendance maximisation under the breakeven constraint, can also be represented in Figure 4.3 by drawing the indifference curves of the fans' aggregate utility function. Assuming that attendances are positively affected by a team's talents and

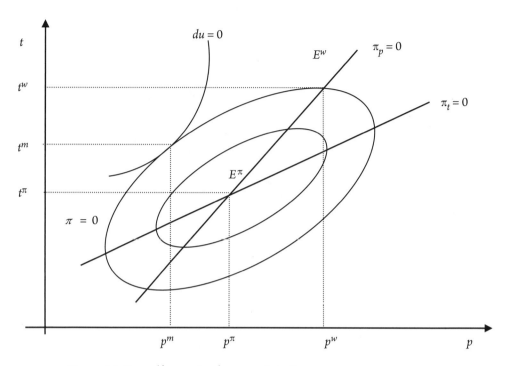

Figure 4.3 Fan welfare or attendance maximisation

negatively affected by the ticket price, maximum fan welfare is then found at the point of tangency between the zero-profit contour $(d\pi = 0)$ and the highest indifference curve $(du = 0)$, which is a point that is far north-west on the zero-profit contour. This club objective will result in a lower ticket price (p^m) than under profit or win maximisation, and the number of talents (t^m) hired by a fan-welfare-maximising club will be lower than the number of talents under win maximisation and higher than under profit maximisation, as can be seen in Figure 4.3.

4.3 Maximum ticket price

In a two-decision variable model, the impact of a **maximum ticket price** is different from its impact in the one-decision variable model of Chapter 2. In Figure 4.4 with first-order conditions $\pi_p = 0$ and $\pi_t = 0$, the **profit-maximising** ticket price and talent demand are determined by the point of intersection E_1^{π}. The maximum ticket price can be represented by the vertical line at the price level p_m. By fixing the price, the locus $\pi_p = 0$ is no longer relevant, so the new optimum is found at the point of intersection E_2^{π} of the vertical p_m line and the locus $\pi_t = 0$. As can be seen, the demand for talent will be lower.

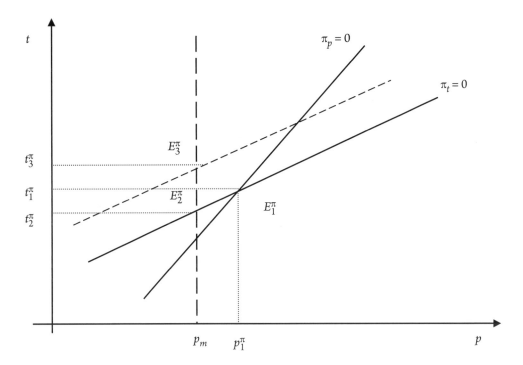

Figure 4.4 Maximum ticket price and profit maximisation

The impact of the maximum ticket price on stadium attendance will depend on the values of the price elasticity and the talent elasticity of demand. Even if the total number of spectators in the stadium is not affected, imposing maximum ticket prices can change the composition of the spectators, because a lower price will probably attract the more price-elastic low-income people, and a lower winning percentage will discourage the more win-elastic supporters. In any case, owner profits in E_2^π will be lower than in E_1^π.

So far, we have assumed that the salary level is an exogenously given constant in this model. With an **endogenous salary level**, a lower demand for talent of all clubs, caused by the maximum ticket price, will also lower the salary level in a competitive player market. A decrease in the salary level causes an upward shift of the locus $\pi_t = 0$, so the impact of imposing a maximum ticket price on the hiring of talent becomes theoretically indeterminate. The final effect depends on the level of the maximum ticket price that is imposed, and on the flexibility of the salary level. In Figure 4.4, the case is shown of a relatively large salary decrease, so that the final equilibrium point is E_3^π, with a higher demand for talent t_3^π.

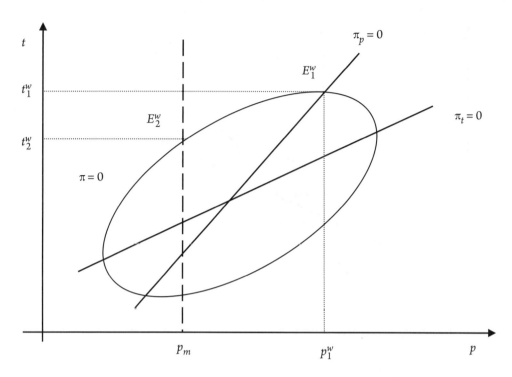

Figure 4.5 Maximum ticket price and win maximisation

Because attendance and club revenue depend on both ticket price and talent, it is also unclear what the impact of a maximum ticket price is on club revenue and profits.

If a team is a win maximiser, facing a breakeven constraint, the equilibrium, without the maximum ticket price, is indicated by point E_1^w in Figure 4.5. If a maximum ticket price is imposed, the new equilibrium is found in point E_2^w at the intersection of the maximum-price line and the zero-profit contour.

With an exogenously given and constant player salary level, it follows that the demand for talent will be reduced. Note that the imposed maximum price can also be too low for the club to stay in business. This happens if the price line is to the left of the zero-profit contour.

4.4 Stadium capacity constraint

We derived in Chapter 2 that a club owner, facing a stadium capacity constraint, charges a higher ticket price than without the constraint. The question is whether that is still true if the owner has to decide simultaneously on the hiring of talent. A stadium capacity restriction can be written as:

$$A[m, p, t] \leq A^{\circ},$$

where A° is the capacity of the stadium. To add this restriction to the p–t diagram, we need the inverse demand function:

$$t = A^{-1}[m, p, A^{\circ}].$$

In this function, the relationship between talent and ticket price is clearly positive, because the ticket price has a negative effect on demand, and a positive effect on the inverse demand. Given the properties of the ticket demand function, this restriction is a non-linear convex function. Nevertheless, there isn't a problem finding a unique point of tangency with the iso-profit contours (see Késenne and Pauwels, 2006). Therefore the restriction is simply drawn as a linear curve in Figure 4.6 where only the points below the curve are feasible. Because the constraint is binding for a **profit-maximising team**, the new equilibrium is found at the point of tangency between this restriction and the highest possible iso-profit curve, which is in point a.

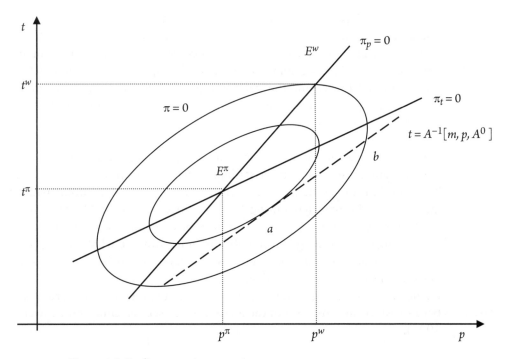

Figure 4.6 Stadium capacity constraint

However, the position of that point depends on the slope of the capacity constraint, and this slope depends on the price and the talent elasticities of the ticket demand function. Therefore, the impact of a stadium capacity constraint on both the ticket price and the talent demand is theoretically indeterminate.

For a **win-maximising team**, the impact of a capacity constraint is different. Because there are again two constraints to the maximisation of the winning percentage, the zero-profit contour and the stadium capacity constraint, the optimal ticket price and talent demand can be found at the upper point of intersection of the two constraints, which is point *b* in Figure 4.6. It follows that the demand for talent will be lower under the capacity constraint. The optimal ticket price can be higher or lower, depending on the stadium capacity constraint. The more limited the stadium capacity, the further south-east the curve shifts.

It is possible that a club's stadium will be too small for all the spectators who want to attend the game if a low maximum ticket price is imposed. In that case, the profit-maximising team faces two constraints, the maximum ticket price and the stadium capacity.

In Figure 4.7, these constraints can be represented by the vertical ticket price line and the dotted line of the stadium capacity constraint. Without the maximum ticket price, the stadium capacity constraint would not be binding, because the initial equilibrium point is below the capacity line. With both the maximum ticket price and the stadium capacity constraint, the new profit-maximising equilibrium is found at E_3, the point of intersection of the two constraints.

Under win maximisation, a team's equilibrium point is also E_3 if both a maximum ticket price and a stadium capacity constraint are in place. This equilibrium point is clearly within the zero-profit contour, which implies that the win-maximising team will become profitable, even if it is not interested in making profits. If both ticket price and talent demand are coming down, it is again theoretically indeterminate what will happen to attendance. With an endogenous salary level which is coming down given the reduction in talent demand, the final effect on the demand for talent of imposing a maximum ticket price is theoretically indeterminate because of the upward shift of the locus $\pi_t = 0$ (see Késenne and Pauwels, 2006).

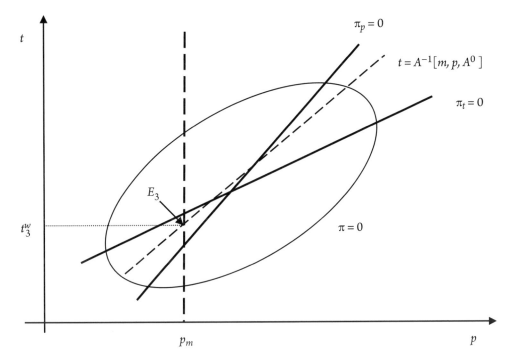

Figure 4.7 Maximum ticket price and stadium capacity constraint

4.5   Numerical example

A simulation with a simplified model can illustrate some of the results in this chapter. Starting from the following attendance function:

$$A = \{\ln(1 + t) - p\}m,$$

the profit function can be written as:

$$\pi = \{p\ln(1 + t) - p^2\}m - ct - c^\circ.$$

Assuming for simplicity that $m = 1$ and $c^0 = 0$, the first-order conditions for **maximum profits** are:

$$\pi_p = \ln(1 + t) - 2p = 0$$

$$\pi_t = \frac{p}{1 + t} - c = 0,$$

which can also be written as:

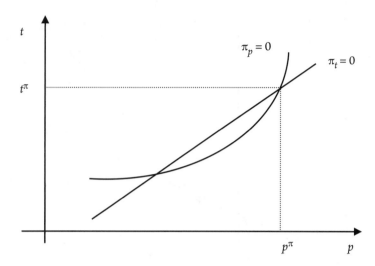

Figure 4.8 First-order conditions for profit maximisation

$$p = \frac{\ln(1 + t)}{2}$$

$$p = c(1 + t).$$

The first relationship between the two decision variables is non-linear; the second is linear.

The non-linear and the linear curve have two points of intersection, as can be seen in Figure 4.8, but only one of these points satisfies the second-order condition, that is, where the slope of $\pi_p = 0$ is steeper than the slope of $\pi_t = 0$.

Lowering the salary level increases the slope of the linear curve $\pi_t = 0$, so the optimal ticket price and talent demand are also higher.

Under **win maximisation**, the breakeven condition $p \ln(1 + t) - p^2 - ct = 0$ must hold, so, after substituting the pricing rule, $p = \frac{\ln(1 + t)}{2}$, which is the same one as under profit maximisation, into the budget constraint, one finds that $p = \sqrt{ct}$.

With these equations the model can be solved for profit and win maximisation. In Table 4.1 the simulation results are given for the profit- and the win-maximisation cases and for two different levels of salary, which is the exogenous variable in this model. As can be seen in the first two columns,

Table 4.1 Simulation: profit versus win maximisation

Salary level	Profit maximisation	Win maximisation	Profit maximisation	Win maximisation	Win maximisation, stadium capacity = 1.0
	0.08	0.08	0.10	0.10	0.10
Talents	17	50	12	30	20
Ticket price	1.5	2	1.3	1.7	2
Payroll	1.4	4	1.2	3	2
Attendances	1.4	1.9	1.2	1.7	1
Revenue	2.1	4	1.6	3	2
Profits	0.7	0	0.4	0	0

both the ticket price and the demand for talent are higher in the win-maximisation case. This confirms the results above. For this particular ticket demand function, attendance and total revenue are also higher in the win-maximisation case.

The third and the fourth columns show that a higher salary level causes a lower optimal ticket price in both scenarios. It also reduces attendance, revenue, cost and profit for this particular revenue function, but this is not necessarily true for a more general specification of the revenue function.

In the last column, it is assumed that the stadium capacity constraint is 1 for the win-maximising club, with the exogenous salary level equal to 0.10. This constraint clearly lowers the talent demand as derived above. For this particular model specification, it also lowers the ticket price.

4.1 Assume that the profit function in a two-decision variable model can be written as:

$$\pi = \frac{p\sqrt{t}}{2} - t - p.$$

Calculate the profit-maximising ticket price and talent demand. What will the optimal number of talents be if a maximum ticket price of 6 euros is imposed by the league?

4.2 Assume that the ticket demand function of a win-maximising club is given by: $A = 20\frac{\sqrt{t}}{p}$ and the stadium can accommodate no more than ten spectators. How many talents will be hired if the maximum ticket price of 8 euros is imposed?

5

Restrictions on player mobility

5.1   Introduction

One regulation system that existed and, to a certain extent, still exists in US
and European professional team sports is the so-called transfer system. In the
US major leagues, it was called the reserve clause or the reservation system,
abolished in the mid-1970s. In European football, it was called the (retain-
and-)transfer system, which was abolished by the famous Bosman verdict
of the European Court of Justice (1995). Without going into the details of
the existing transfer systems, and the institutional differences between the
US and Europe, the basic characteristic was that players were owned by a
club for the length of their career. Players were not free to move to another
club even at the end of their contract. A player could change clubs only if the
old and the new club reached an agreement on a transfer fee. So, players and
player contracts were traded between clubs on the transfer market like, albeit
well-paid, modern slaves. If a player, at the end of his contract, did not agree
to the conditions of the new contract that was offered to him, or if he did
not want to move to the other club, his only option was to end his career as
a professional player. Some monopoly leagues have tried to give this clearly
illegal system a legal character by asserting that players were employed by the
league and not by the clubs. A club was only a branch of a large multi-plant
company, and players were delegated by the league to the clubs. However,
when they started to realise the consequences of this argument, such as also
taking responsibility for all the financial losses and debts of the clubs, they
quickly dropped the whole idea. Only the US soccer league still tries to stick
to this scenario, which will certainly not last.

Although football players, at the end of their contract, are now free world-
wide and the existing transfer systems are no longer in place, the player
labour markets are still troubled by all kinds of attempts of clubs and leagues
to limit the free movement of players. One of these attempts is the FIFA–
EU Transfer Agreement (2001), where a complex compensation system for

youth training was installed, which is little less than an attempt to introduce the transfer fee by the back door by giving it another name. Clubs also reacted by lengthening player contracts, so the buying and selling of contract players on the transfer market simply continued. Some players were also forced to sign a new contract with their club before the old contract expired. So, players might be free at the end of their contract, but some would never reach the end of their contract.

The main argument to justify the introduction of a transfer system in professional team sports has always been that it is necessary for a sports league to have a reasonably balanced competition. If players are free to move to the team of their choice, they will choose the best-paying team. As a consequence, the best players all end up in the richest clubs, killing the uncertainty of outcome in the league, with the result that public interest fades. Another reason is that a transfer system helps to keep top player salaries down and increases a club's profit. In a free market, top players can sell their talents to the highest bidder. A transfer system allows club owners to capture the rents. A more positive effect of a transfer system is that player salaries will be more in line with a player's value to the league, rather than with his value to the club. This way, a transfer system provides compensation for the inherent negative external effects that teams cause to each other by hiring players away from other teams (see Noll, 1974a).

More or less the same arguments are used to justify the so-called **rookie draft** in the US major leagues. Basically, this system comes down to a reverse-order-of-finish draft, where the lowest-ranked team in the previous season is the first to select the best young college player. The team with the best record is the last to pick a rookie. To prevent perverse effects and moral hazard, that is, low-ranked teams who intentionally lose end-of-season games in order to have the first pick, leagues have introduced a lottery system for the first round of picks. Like a transfer system, a rookie draft system also allows the financially poor teams to compete with the rich teams for new talent, so that the competitive balance in a league improves (see Kahane, 2006).

In this chapter, we will analyse the impact of a transfer system on the competitive balance and player salary levels in a Walras equilibrium model. Again, we will consider both the profit and the win maximisation cases. Section 5.5 discusses the impact of the increased international mobility of players between nationally protected product markets.

5.2 The transfer system in a profit-maximisation league

If clubs are profit maximisers, and club owners are aware of the detrimental effect of unbalanced competition, a free market for players will be self-regulating, because it is in each team's own interest that it does not become too dominant. Hence restrictions to player mobility are not necessary. Moreover, based on the Coase theorem (1960), the so-called 'invariance proposition' states that, if clubs are profit maximisers, restrictions on the player labour market, such as a transfer system or a rookie draft, do not change the distribution of playing talent among clubs in a league compared with a competitive, free agency player market. If a player is worth more to a large-market club than to a small-market club, both clubs will easily come to an agreement to trade that player on the transfer market. The large club is willing to pay a transfer fee that is lower than the value of the player for the large club. The small club is also willing to accept a transfer fee that is higher than the value of that player for the small club. This view goes back to the seminal article on the economics of professional team sports by Rottenberg (1956). Later on, this proposition was formally proven by Quirk and El-Hodiri (1974).

Hence, with or without the transfer system, a player will end up in the team where his productivity is highest. This can be shown graphically in Figure 5.1, which reproduces the Walras competitive market equilibrium of Chapter 3. Assume that the actual distribution of talent differs from the competitive market equilibrium, say t^a. At this point, the marginal revenue of talent is much higher in the large club then in the small club, $mr_x > mr_y$. Both profit-maximising clubs can increase their profits by trading players; that is, playing talent will be sold by the small club to the large clubs until the difference between the marginal revenues is eliminated, and thus, in Figure 5.1, t^a moves to the right until it reaches t^π. So, the final outcome will be the same as the free market outcome. What is different from the free market outcome is that the small-market club receives a transfer fee for the players who are sold to the large-market club, so the small-market club's revenue is higher. The extra revenue, however, does not change the marginal revenue of talent, so the talent demand curves do not shift. The transfer money only increases the profits, or lowers the losses, of the small-market club.

In the US, where the player reservation system in the major leagues was abolished in the mid-1970s, the empirical evidence shows that there exists no correlation whatsoever between the restrictions on the player market and the competitive balance in a league. On the contrary, there is some empirical

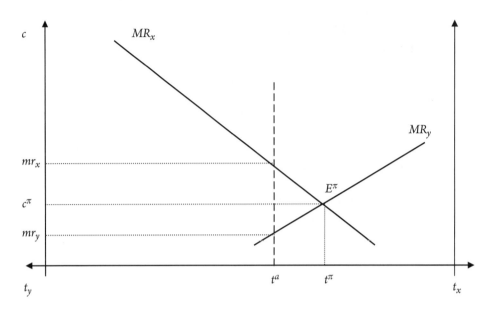

Figure 5.1 The transfer system in a profit-maximisation league

research showing an improvement of the competitive balance since the intro-duction of free agency (see Quirk and Fort, 1992).

To a certain extent, the transfer system has functioned as a kind of redistri-bution system; it increased the financial security of the small-market clubs that could reserve their talented players, on the one hand, or sell them for a transfer fee, on the other hand. Small-market clubs were clearly net sellers of talent on the transfer market. The existence of the transfer system has also tempted small-market clubs to invest more in youth training, because the most talented players could be sold on the transfer market.

How does a transfer market affect the player salaries in a profit maximisation league? The player market in professional team sports under the transfer system is often cited as the classical textbook example of a monopsony. A monopsonised labour market is a market where there is just one agent on the demand side, or only one employer. If players are owned by a club, or if players, owing to monopoly league regulations, are not free to choose their employer, or if they are allowed to move to another club only if both clubs agree on the transfer fee, each club, or the league as a cartel of clubs, can be considered as the sole employer of professional players (see Rottenberg, 1956). Because a monopsonist is facing an upward-sloping market supply of talent, a club is no longer a wage taker on the talent market. Monopsony power allows wage setting in order to maximise profits. At the profit-maximising point, where

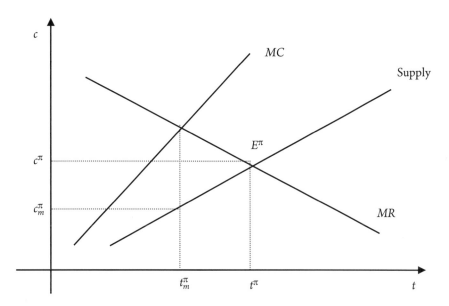

Figure 5.2 Monopsony under profit maximisation

marginal revenue equals marginal cost, the wage level, set by a monopsonist, is below marginal revenue.

This can be shown graphically. Assume that there is only one employer on the player market, which can be the league or the club. This single employer is facing the market supply of talent, which is assumed to be upward sloping. The supply curve is shown in Figure 5.2. Assume that the demand curve for talent of a profit maximiser is given by the marginal revenue curve MR. Talent will be hired until marginal revenue equals marginal cost. But what is the marginal cost of talent for a non-discriminating monopsonist? If a monopsonist wants to hire one more talent he has to pay a higher cost for that extra talent, because the market supply curve is upward sloping. But, in the case of non-discrimination, that same higher salary level has to be paid to all talents who were previously hired. This will increase the marginal cost of talent by much more than just the salary of that extra playing talent. As a consequence, the marginal cost of talent (MC) can be represented in Figure 5.2 by an upward-sloping curve, above and steeper than the market supply curve. Equalising MR and MC, a profit maximiser will hire t_m^π talents, but he will pay only salary level c_m^π, because that is all he needs to pay in order to attract t_m^π talents. Comparing this outcome with the free market outcome, where market demand equals market supply at point E^π, with talent employment t^π and unit cost of talent c^π, a monopsonist hires fewer playing talents and pays lower salaries. More important is that the salary level paid in a monopsonistic player market is below marginal revenue. The conclusion is that, under a transfer system, players are exploited by the cartel of profit-maximising clubs.

More formally, this conclusion can be derived as follows, starting again from the clubs' revenue function and cost function, as specified in Chapter 3:

$$R_i = R_i[m_i, t_i] \quad \text{and} \quad C_i = ct_i + c_i^0.$$

If the league, as a cartel of clubs, behaves as a monopsonist on the player labour market, its season revenue (R) and cost (C) function can be written as:

$$R[m, t] \quad \text{and} \quad C = ct + c^0,$$

with:

$$m = \sum_i^n m_i \qquad t = \sum_i^n t_i \qquad c^0 = \sum_i^n c_i^0.$$

In this approach, the unit cost of a playing talent also includes the transfer fee paid minus the (expected) transfer fee received when the talent moves to another club. However, in a closed league with a fixed talent supply, the sum of all transfer fees paid by the clubs has to equal the sum of all transfer fees received by the clubs, so the unit cost of playing talent is not affected by the transfer fees. All transfer money stays within the league's money circuit.

Because the league is the sole demander of playing talent, it faces the market supply of talent, which is an upward-sloping function of the salary level:

$$c = c[t] \quad \text{with} \quad \frac{\partial c}{\partial t} > 0. \tag{5.1}$$

In a profit-maximising league, the optimality condition states that playing talent is hired until marginal revenue equals marginal cost. For a non-discriminating monopsonist, facing an upward-sloping market supply curve, the marginal labour cost will be higher than the salary level, which is no longer constant. So, the optimality condition, $MR = MC$, can be written as:

$$\frac{\partial R}{\partial t} = c + \frac{\partial c}{\partial t} t. \tag{5.2}$$

From (5.1) and (5.2), it can be seen that the salary level is below marginal revenue, so the players are exploited by the owners in a profit-maximising league. It goes without saying that this monopsonistic exploitation of players under the transfer system also increases owner profits.

This theoretical result for the player salary level is also supported by empirical research. Scully (1974, 1989) estimated the marginal revenue of major league baseball (MLB) players in the US in a two-step procedure. In a first step, he calculated a player's contribution to his team's winning percentage, which can be easily observed in baseball, where individual performances count more than in other team sports. In a second step, he used an econometric model to estimate the partial effect of the winning percentage on club revenue. From these figures, Scully estimated what he called the rate of monopsonistic exploitation: $RME = 1 - \frac{c}{MR}$. Scully's results were striking. Before the mid-1970s, he found a considerable degree of exploitation of MLB players in the US. After the mid-1970s, the introduction of free agency caused a tremendous increase in player salaries when the players managed to capture their legitimate share of the huge owner profits, and the underpayment of baseball players in the US came to an end. In a new investigation, Scully (1999) found that players were more or less paid according to their marginal revenue. These observations confirm what can be derived from economic theory.

Moreover, Feess and Muehlheusser (2003a, 2003b) conclude from their theoretical model that the abolition of the transfer system in European football by the Bosman verdict of the European Court of Justice (1995) can have a favourable effect on investment in training, player effort and expected social welfare, and also that the FIFA–EU Transfer Agreement (2001), reintroducing compensation for youth training, has turned the clock back by diminishing incentives to invest in the education of young talent.

5.3 The transfer system in a win-maximisation league

What is the impact of the transfer system on competitive balance and player salaries in a win-maximisation league? As seen before, the demand curves for talent of win-maximising clubs are given by the net average revenue (NAR) curves, presented in Figure 5.3, with E^w as the competitive market equilibrium. Starting again from a different distribution of talent t^a with unit cost of talent c^w, it is clear that the small-market club loses money, because the unit cost of talent c^w is higher than the net average revenue nar_y. The large-market club is profitable because its average revenue nar_x is higher than the unit cost of talent. If both clubs' objective is to maximise their own winning percentage under the breakeven constraint, the large-market club will try to buy more playing talents and the small-market club will want to sell talents on the transfer market. Again the distribution of talent t^a moves in the direction of the free market distribution t^w.

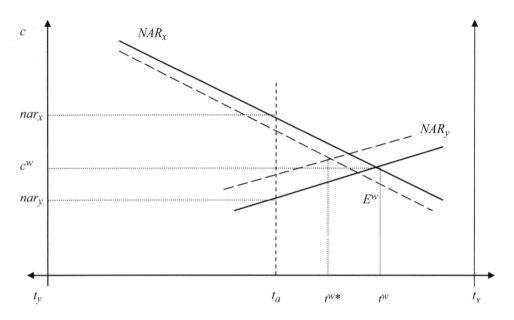

Figure 5.3 The transfer system in a win-maximisation league

There is an important difference, however, with the profit-maximisation scenario. Because the small-market club receives a transfer fee for the players it sells to the large-market clubs, its net average revenue goes up, and it will use the money to increase the demand for talent. Hence, the upward shift of the small club's average revenue curve and, consequently, the downward shift of the large-market club's average revenue curve will result in an improved competitive balance in the league, indicated by t^{w*} (see Lavoie, 2000). The crucial question, however, is how significant this shift will be. It would be significant if the initial distribution of playing talent, that is, before clubs start to trade players on the transfer market, was more equal. But this is not the case, certainly not in Europe, where there is no rookie draft system. By definition, a small-market club is a club with a weak drawing potential, not only for spectators, but also for players, so the initial player market equilibrium under free agency is already showing an unequal distribution of talent. It follows that there is little to trade between the small- and the large-market clubs, so the distribution of talent under a transfer system will be close to the talent distribution in a competitive labour market. Only occasionally, a star player can be sold by the small-market club, which will allow that club to attract one or two regular players instead. Empirical research has shown that this effect is indeed rather insignificant (see Szymanski and Kuypers, 1999). The conclusion is that, in a win-maximisation league, the transfer system can have only a small

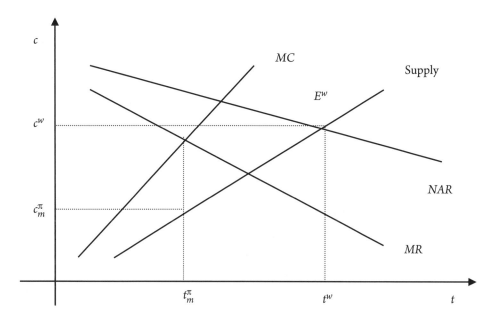

Figure 5.4 Monopsony under win maximisation

positive effect on the distribution of talent among teams and the competitive balance in a league.

One of the implications of this result is that the combination of a transfer system and a rookie draft system, in a league with win-maximising clubs, could have a more significant positive effect on the competitive balance. A reverse-order-of-finish draft can bring about a more equal initial distribution of talent, before the buying and the selling of players on the transfer market start.

In order to analyse the effect of a transfer system on the player salary level, we start again from the monopsony model of the player labour market. If all clubs in a league are win maximisers, hiring as many talents as possible within the limits of their budgets, the league, as a monopsonist, can be assumed to maximise the total number of talents. Playing talent will be hired until all league revenue is spent on salaries. It follows that the equilibrium point is found at the intersection of the market supply curve and the net average revenue curve (E^w), as can be seen in Figure 5.4. The salary paid by the talent-maximising and non-discriminating monopsonist has to be c^w. This salary level is clearly above marginal revenue, which means that players in a talent-maximising league, as distinct from a profit-maximising league, are not exploited by the monopsonist. On average, players are even overpaid.

Moreover, the average salary level is the same as in a competitive labour market, where the equilibrium is found at the point of intersection of market demand and market supply (E^w). As a consequence, the abolition of the transfer system in a talent-maximising league does not allow any rise in average player salaries.

More formally, the objective of the talent-maximising monopsonist can be written as:

$$\text{Max } t \quad \text{subject to:} \quad R[m{\cdot}t] - c[t]t - c^0 = 0,$$

where c^0 can also include a certain profit amount. The first-order conditions for talent maximisation can then be written as:

$$\frac{\partial R}{\partial t} = c + \frac{\partial c}{\partial t}t - \frac{1}{\lambda} \tag{5.3}$$

$$\frac{R - c^0}{t} = c, \tag{5.4}$$

where λ is the positive Lagrange multiplier. The first equation shows that the marginal revenue is lower than the marginal cost of talent, so a talent-maximising league hires more playing talents than a profit-maximising league. The second equation indicates that the demand for talent is given by the net average revenue function. In order to show that players are no longer exploited by the monopsonist, but rather overpaid, we start from the definition of the average net revenue (NAR), which can be rewritten as:

$$R = \left(\frac{R - c^0}{t}\right)t + c^0, \quad \text{so } MR = NAR + \frac{\partial NAR}{\partial t}t.$$

If $\frac{\partial(NAR)}{\partial t} < 0$, net average revenue is above marginal revenue, and so, according to (5.4), the unit cost of talent, or the player salary level, is above marginal revenue, which would mean that players are on average overpaid in a win-maximisation league.

However, the unit cost of talent in a win-maximisation league c_w can also be below the marginal revenue of talent, depending on the size of the wage/turnover ratio ct_i/R_i. If the wage/turnover ratio is very low, or $c_i^0 + \pi_i^0$ is very high, players can also be underpaid in a win-maximisation league.

By definition, it holds that $R_i = NAR_it_i + c_i^0 + \pi_i^0$. Taking the first derivative with respect to talent, we find that:

$$MR_i = \frac{\partial R_i}{\partial t_i} = NAR_i + t_i \frac{\partial NAR_i}{\partial t_i}.$$

Because $\frac{\partial NAR_i}{\partial t_i} = \frac{\partial AR_i}{\partial t_i} + \frac{c_i^0 + \pi_i^0}{t_i^2}$ can be positive or negative, it follows that the unit cost of talent under win maximisation $c_w (=NAR_i)$ can be above or below the marginal revenue MR_i (see Késenne, 2010).

Discriminating monopsonists

Monopsonists also have the power to discriminate among players, so one cannot exclude that some players, like Jean-Marc Bosman, are underpaid and exploited. A discriminating monopsonist does not pay every playing talent the same salary level. One possibility is that a discriminating monopsonist pays only the salary level he needs to pay given the market supply conditions. Facing an upward-sloping supply curve, he has to pay a higher salary to every newly hired talent, but he can discriminate because he does not have to pay that same higher salary to all previously hired talent. It follows that, in the **profit-maximisation** case, the curve of the marginal cost of talent converges to the supply curve of talent, so the profit-maximising equilibrium is found at point E^π of Figure 5.2. Although this point is the same as the competitive market equilibrium, it does not mean that there is no exploitation of players. Only the last talent hired is paid according to its marginal revenue; all other playing talents are paid below marginal revenue.

Under win maximisation, discriminating monopsonists will hire more talents than t^w in Figure 5.4, because they are paying a lower salary to all talents hired before the last one, with the result that they can use the exploitation money to hire more talents.

5.4   Youth training compensation and the freedom to move

When the transfer system in European football was abolished by the Bosman verdict in 1995, sports clubs and federations were concerned about youth training. Obviously, youth training in sports is important, and clubs should be encouraged and compensated for the training costs. However, this reasonable principle does not necessarily imply that, in sports, the European laws of free movement of workers should be violated. It is perfectly possible to meet both concerns of the European Court: the free movement of players *and* the encouragement and compensation of youth training. The court could have disentangled the compensation of youth training and the movement of a player to another team. It is not necessary to link the two. The training of a young player should be compensated for in any case, whether the player stays or leaves. The league can set up a youth training compensation fund, with financial contributions from all clubs as a percentage of their budget. The league should then redistribute this money depending on the quantity and quality of the clubs' youth training and development. This way, a club is compensated for the cost of training young players without any restriction on the free movement of players. Given that the amount of money that can be redistributed from the fund is fixed, the clubs have to compete with one another for a larger share of the fund, which will create a strong incentive to invest in youth training. Depending on the percentage of the clubs' budgets that has to be contributed to the fund, very large amounts of money can be collected. If youth training, in the eyes of the football leagues, is important enough to violate fundamental European laws, the leagues should also set this percentage high enough to meet their objective of more youth training.

A simple mathematical model can show the most important consequences of this youth training compensation system. Assume that there are n clubs in a league and that each club's revenues (R_i) depend on the size of its market (m_i) and on its winning percentage (w_i). Furthermore, each club contributes the same percentage μ of its budget to a youth training fund. The collected money of the fund then equals $\mu \sum_j^n R_j$, which is redistributed according to the clubs' relative effort to train young talent. Each club receives a share s_i from the fund. Under these assumptions, after-sharing club revenue (R^*) can be written as:

$$R_i^* = (1 - \mu)R_i + s_i\mu \sum_j^n R_j \text{ or } R_i^* = (1-\mu)R_i + ns_i\mu\bar{R} \text{ with } \sum_j^n s_j = 1,$$

if $s_i = 1/n$, that is, if each club puts the same effort into youth training, $ns_i = 1$, and $R_i^* = (1 - \mu)R_i + \mu\bar{R}$, that is, each club receives the same amount of money $\mu\bar{R}$ from the fund. But large-budget clubs have contributed a larger amount. Indeed, if $R_i > \bar{R}$, it can be derived that $R_i^* < R_i$.

The ex-post budget of a small club (with $R_i < \bar{R}$) will be higher than its ex-ante budget, because it receives more money from the fund than it has contributed.

In general, the budgets of small and large clubs, before and after youth compensation, will be the same if their share of effort in youth training is the same as their budget share, that is, if $s_i = \frac{R_i}{\sum R_j} = \frac{R_i}{n\bar{R}}$. So, a club will see its budget go up if $s_i > \frac{R_i}{n\bar{R}}$. The league should also put the clubs' contribution to the training fund (μ) high enough for the compensation the clubs receive for their training efforts to be high enough to cover the costs of training. This way more money becomes available for hiring talent.

Because it is also a revenue-sharing arrangement, this youth training compensation will have consequences for the distribution of talent and the competitive balance in a league. Under the more realistic assumption that European football clubs are win maximisers, under a given budget constraint which is not necessarily the breakeven constraint, this compensation system will improve the competitive balance in a league if all clubs put the same effort into youth training.

If stars indicate ex-post (after-sharing) values of the variables, the ex-post club revenue can be written as:

$$R_i^* = (1 - \mu)R_i + ns_i \mu \bar{R} \text{ with } \sum_j^n s_j = 1.$$

If teams are win maximisers, their demand for talent is determined by the net average revenue, that is, after subtraction of the cost of training $C_{tr}[s_i]$, which depends on the training effort s_i. If a team is not interested in making profits, but wants to maximise playing success, its demand for playing talent is not determined by the marginal revenue of talent, but by the average revenue of talent, or, after subtraction of other costs, by the net average revenue (NAR):

$$NAR_i^* = \frac{1}{t_i}\{(1 - \mu)R_i + ns_i \mu \bar{R} - C_{tr}[s_i]\}.$$

The impact of a change in the parameter μ on the demand for talent can be derived by considering:

$$\frac{\partial NAR_i^*}{\partial \mu} = \frac{1}{t_i}[ns_i \bar{R} - R_i].$$

So, if $s_i = 1/n$:
$$\frac{\partial NAR_i^*}{\partial \mu} = \frac{1}{t_i}[\bar{R} - R_i].$$

It can now be seen that $\frac{\partial NAR_i^*}{\partial \mu} > 0$ if $R_i < \bar{R}$, so small-budget clubs will increase their demand for talent if the percentage (μ) of the contribution to the training fund goes up. Because the opposite happens to the large-budget clubs (with $R_i > \bar{R}$), the competitive balance in the league will improve. The more small teams invest in training, compared to the large teams, the more the competitive balance will improve.

5.5 International player mobility (*)

In most industries, one observes a very intensive international trade of goods and services and mobility of capital. Labour, however, is internationally quite immobile. Since the Second World War, the European Union has been created, with a common market, one single currency and one central bank. Although the European labour market has been officially deregulated as well, the international mobility of labour clearly lags behind. In the professional sports industry, however, one observes a very high degree of international player mobility, while the product market is still closed and nationally protected. The Bosman verdict of the European Court of Justice (1995) abolished not only the transfer system for end-of-contract players, but also any restriction on the number of foreign European players who can be fielded. That ruling has caused a tremendous increase in international player mobility. The best players of the small and poor countries moved to the rich teams in the large and wealthy countries. Meanwhile, the national product markets are still closed. All clubs have to play in their own national championships, which differ enormously in club and league budgets. As a consequence, the teams of small countries have to compete for the best players in an open European labour market with the teams of large countries with budgets that are more than ten times greater. At the same time, the teams in small countries are not allowed to participate in the rich national championships of the large countries, or to compete in an open European product market.

In this section, using a simplified **two-country/four-team model** with quadratic club revenue functions, we analyse how the competitive balance is affected if one moves from nationally protected labour and product markets to an internationally open labour and product market. Because this model applies to Europe, rather than to the US sports markets, we assume that clubs are win maximisers. Other approaches can be found in Provost (2003), Haan et al. (2005) and Goossens and Késenne (2007).

Assume that there are two countries: A is the large country with national market size m_A, and B is the small country with market size m_B, with $m = m_A + m_B$. There are two clubs in each country: club x is the large-market club, and club y is the small-market club. The national markets are divided over the two clubs' local markets, so $m_A = m_{Ax} + m_{Ay}$ and $m_B = m_{Bx} + m_{By}$, with $m_A > m_B$, $m_{Ax} > m_{Ay}$ and $m_{Bx} > m_{By}$.

We further assume that the following condition is fulfilled:

$$m_{Ax} - m_{Bx} < m_{ix} - m_{iy} \quad \text{for } i = A, B. \tag{5.5}$$

This condition states that the difference between the market sizes of the two large-market clubs is smaller than the difference between the market sizes of the large- and small-market clubs in each country. This condition is clearly fulfilled in the European countries.

The season revenue of a club depends on three important factors: the size of its market, its winning percentage and the uncertainty of outcome. For each club j in country i, we specify the revenue function as follows:

$$R_{ij} = (m_{ij} + m_i/2)w_{ij} - \beta w_{ij}^2 \quad \text{for } i = A, B \quad \text{and} \quad \text{for } j = x, y. \quad (5.6)$$

The revenue of a club depends not only on the number of stadium spectators in its local market but, increasingly, on broadcasting and commercial revenue like sponsorship, merchandising and licensing. Because these revenue sources tend to be determined by the size of the national market, they are captured by m_i divided by the number of clubs.

The winning percentage of each team in each country is indicated by w_{ij} and is defined by:

$$w_{ij} = \frac{t_{ij}}{t_{ix} + t_{iy}} = \frac{t_{ij}}{t_i},$$

where t_{ij} is the number of playing talents of team j in country i, and t_i is the supply of talent (or the sum of talents) in country i. We assume that the supply of talent in each country can be changed only by international player mobility. The total supply of talent in both countries together is assumed to be constant and equal to t_s.

On the cost side, we consider player cost to be the sole cost of production:

$$C_{ij} = c_i t_{ij}.$$

The unit cost of talent is the same for both clubs in each country, but differs between countries.

5.5.1 Closed national product and labour markets

The benchmark model is a closed league in each country; both the product market and the labour market are nationally protected, each club plays in its own national championship, and there are no international transfers of players. In that scenario, we start from the basic assumption that the initial competitive balance *between* the two nations is given by their relative market size:

$$\frac{t_A}{t_B} = \frac{m_A}{m_B}. \tag{5.7}$$

We assume all professional football clubs in Europe to be win maximisers under the breakeven constraint, so their demand curve for talent is given by the average revenue. Even if the average revenue of each club apparently depends on the number of playing talents hired by its opponent, the non-cooperative Nash equilibrium reduces to a Walras equilibrium, because the supply of talent is fixed in a closed league (see Chapter 3). Assuming that the unit cost of talent in each country is c_i, the competitive balance can be derived from $AR_{ix} = c_i = AR_{iy}$ or:

$$(m_{ix} + m_i/2) - \beta w_{ix} = (m_{iy} + m_i/2) - bw_{iy} \quad \text{for } i = A, B,$$

so:

$$w_{ix} - w_{iy} = \frac{m_{ix} - m_{iy}}{\beta}. \tag{5.8}$$

It follows that the club with the largest local market also has the best-performing team.

If the closed labour market in each country is competitive, with a fixed supply of talent t_i, the equilibrium salary level in each country can also be found. The average revenue functions of the two clubs in each country can be rewritten as:

$$m_{ix} + m_i/2 - \beta w_{ix} = c_i t_i$$

$$m_{iy} + m_i/2 - \beta w_{iy} = c_i t_i.$$

Summing these equations results in: $2m_i - \beta = 2c_i t_i$, so:

$$c_i = \frac{2m_i - \beta}{2t_i}. \tag{5.9}$$

This expression shows that the salary level is negatively related to the supply of talent, and positively to the size of the national market, which affects the demand for talent. Based on ratio (5.7), one can also derive that:

$$c_A > c_B,$$

which means that the salary level per unit of talent in the large country is higher than the salary level in the small country, notwithstanding the fact that a country's (innate) talents are assumed to be proportional to the country's market size, and that both countries show the same preference for balanced competition.

5.5.2   Open labour market and closed product markets

In the second scenario, the labour market is opened so that players can move freely to the club that offers the best salaries, but the national product markets are still closed. This resembles the post-Bosman era in European football, where unlimited international transfers are possible in a common player labour market. With a given unit cost of talent c, the reaction functions are now given by:

$$AR_{ij} = c \qquad \text{for all } i \text{ and } j, \tag{5.10}$$

where c is the unit cost of playing talent in the common market. Notice that in this scenario the supply of talent is flexible in each country.

A first question is how the competitive balance *between* the nations is affected by the deregulation of the labour market. From (5.10), one can derive that:

$$AR_{Ax} + AR_{Ay} = AR_{Bx} + AR_{By} \quad \text{or} \quad \frac{2m_A - \beta}{t_A} = \frac{2m_B - \beta}{t_B},$$

so the new competitive balance between the two countries becomes:

$$\frac{\hat{t}_A}{\hat{t}_B} = \frac{2m_A - \beta}{2m_B - \beta} > \frac{t_A}{t_B} \tag{5.11}$$

Comparing (5.11) to (5.7), it is clear that the gap between the large and the small countries has widened by the deregulation of the player labour market.

A second question is how the competitive balance *within* each national league is affected by the liberalisation of the labour market. Because of the open player market, the supply of talent in each country has now changed to $\hat{t}_A$ and $\hat{t}_B$. Starting again from (5.10), one finds the same competitive balance in both countries as before:

$$\widehat{w}_{ix} - \widehat{w}_{iy} = \frac{m_{ix} - m_{iy}}{\beta} = w_{ix} - w_{iy}.$$

It follows that within the large and the small country the competitive balance has not changed by the deregulation of the player labour market. This does not sound unreasonable, because the competitive balance depends basically on the relative size of the clubs' markets. If a small country loses its best talents, a competitive labour market in that country guarantees that the 'second-best' talents are attracted by the large-market clubs in that country.

A third question is how the (international) market clearing salary level per unit of talent is affected by deregulating the labour market. This salary level $\hat{c}$ can be derived as:

$$\hat{c} = \frac{2m_i - \beta}{2\hat{t}_i} = \frac{m - \beta}{t_s}, \qquad \text{so} \qquad c_A > \hat{c} > c_B. \qquad (5.12)$$

As could be expected, a comparison with the results in (5.9) shows that the market clearing salary level per unit of talent comes down in the large country and goes up in the small country.

5.5.3 Open product and player markets

In a third scenario, we investigate what happens if not only the labour market but also the product market is liberalised. Assume that the opening of the European product market means that the winners (the large-market teams) of each country leave the national championships and are promoted to a European division. Because these teams compete on the European product market, the variables and parameters of the revenue functions change. In revenue function (5.6) the size of the national market m_i has to be replaced by the size of the international market m, which is the sum of m_A and m_B, because these clubs can benefit from the large amounts of European broadcasting and commercial revenue. In revenue function (5.6), the winning percentage also changes, because the large-market clubs play only against each other in a European division. For these clubs, the revenue function becomes:

$$R_{ix} = (m_{ix} + m/2)\frac{t_{ix}}{t_x} - \beta\left(\frac{t_{ix}}{t_x}\right)^2 \qquad \text{for } i = A, B,$$

where the total supply of talent is $t_x = t_{ax} + t_{zx}$. Solving the two reaction equations, one finds the competitive balance between the two large-market clubs:

$$\widetilde{w}_{Ax} - \widetilde{w}_{Bx} = \frac{m_{Ax} - m_{Bx}}{\beta}.$$

Comparing this result with the competitive balances in (5.8) and assuming that condition (5.5) is fulfilled, it can be derived that the competitive balance between the top clubs in the European division is more equal than the balances in the two national divisions before the opening of the product market.

The market clearing salary level can be found to be the same as in (5.12), which indicates that the equilibrium salary level per unit of talent in the

European division will be as high as the salary level before the opening of the product market.

What this chapter shows is that opening the international labour market in the professional team sports industry, with closed national product markets, creates a growing gap between the budget and the performances of the clubs in the large and small countries. Indeed, the deregulation of the European player market by the Bosman verdict of the European Court of Justice (1995) has clearly widened the gap between the football teams in the large and in the small countries. This analysis also shows that the balance can be restored by opening the product market of the European football industry by creating one or more European divisions, where only the best teams of each country meet, while leaving their national championships (see Hoehn and Szymanski, 1999). The existing UEFA Champions League, which is supposed to open the European football market, is actually closing it more than ever by excluding 47 of the 52 European countries the UEFA represents. With very few exceptions, only the clubs from the so-called 'Big Five' countries manage to reach the semi-finals. The only effect of the UEFA Champions League has been a devastating impact on the competitive balance both between and within countries (see Késenne, 2007b).

5.6 Conclusion

A general conclusion from economic theory is that, under the transfer system, players are exploited by profit-maximising club owners, but they are rather overpaid by win-maximising owners. The exploitation hypothesis under profit maximisation was well supported by empirical research. There are also indications that the overpayment of talent under win maximisation is supported by the facts.

Regarding the competitive balance in a league, there is very little theoretical and empirical evidence that a transfer system has had any significant effect on the distribution of talent among teams.

The only advantage of the transfer system is that it enhances the financial position of the small-market clubs, because they are net sellers of talent on the transfer market. It allows these clubs to survive or the increase their profits.

Economic theory also shows that an open European player and product market can close the gap between the large and the small countries that has been created by opening only the European player market.

EXERCISES 5

5.1 Let the revenue function of a non-discriminating monopsonist be given by $R = 2.8t - t^2$. The cost of playing talent is the only cost, and the market supply for talent is given by $c = 0.4 + 0.5t$. What will the equilibrium demand of talent and salary level be if the monopsonist tries to maximise profits? Also calculate the rate of monopsonistic exploitation (RME).

5.2 With the same revenue, cost and supply functions as in exercise 5.1, calculate the equilibrium demand for talent of a discriminating profit-maximising monopsonist.

5.3 With the same revenue, cost and supply functions as in exercise 5.1, but with a win-maximising monopsonist, calculate the equilibrium demand for talent and the salary level of a non-discriminating monopsonist.

6

Revenue sharing

6.1 Introduction

In most professional sports leagues, one or another revenue-sharing arrangement among teams exists. We define revenue sharing as a distribution or redistribution of money in the sense that money that is earned by one team is given to another team. The main objective of revenue sharing is guaranteeing a reasonable competitive balance in a league. Given the peculiarities of the professional team sports industry, it makes sense to share club revenue. If two teams are necessary to play a match, and more teams to organise a championship, all participants should have a share of the success and the revenue of the championship. The fact that a championship consists of home and away games does not undermine this argument. As long as there is no free entry into the market, and relocations of teams are not allowed, the differences in market size and drawing potential of large cities versus small towns yield a lasting advantage to the large-market teams.

The aim of this chapter is to analyse the impact of revenue sharing. Again, we will deal with both the Walras and the Nash equilibrium models and distinguish between profit and win maximisation. Because the distribution of talent in a win-maximisation league is more unequal than in a profit-maximisation league, and salaries are much higher, as derived in Chapter 3, it can be argued that revenue sharing, as well as other regulations to guarantee a reasonable competitive balance and to lower top salary levels, is more needed in a win-maximisation league. We also have to distinguish between different revenue-sharing arrangements, because they can have a different impact.

6.2 Revenue sharing in the Walras equilibrium model

Starting with the Walras equilibrium model, we will first consider the impact of revenue sharing in a profit-maximisation league, followed by its impact in a win-maximisation league.

6.2.1   Revenue sharing in a profit-maximisation league

There are several arrangements to share revenue. In theory, the simplest case is where all club revenues are shared according to a single fixed-share parameter. The reality, however, is more complicated. In some leagues, such as the NFL in North America, the gate receipts of every single match are shared between the home and away teams; in other leagues, only the total season broadcast rights are pooled and shared among all teams. Often the broadcast rights are monopolised and equally redistributed by the league or based on specific criteria. Also, some club revenues, such as local TV rights, are not shared. In most cases, a complex combination of these arrangements exists.

One can derive the impact of revenue sharing by considering a simple two-team league with team revenue functions that depend only on market size and playing talent (see Quirk and Fort, 1992). In the case of a two-team league, the difference between a gate sharing and a pool sharing arrangement is not relevant, because they turn out to be the same arrangement. Let R_x be the season revenue of the large-market club and R_y the season revenue of the small-market club. If a star indicates the after-sharing values and μ is the share parameter, the after-sharing revenues in a simple gate sharing system can be written as:

$$R_x^* = \mu R_x + (1 - \mu) R_y$$

$$R_y^* = \mu R_y + (1 - \mu) R_x \quad \text{with} \quad 0.5 \le \mu < 1. \tag{6.1}$$

Because the demand curve for talent of a profit-maximising team is given by the marginal revenue curve (MR), the clubs' demand curves for talent can be written as:

$$\frac{\partial R_x^*}{\partial t_x} = \mu \frac{\partial R_x}{\partial t_x} + (1 - \mu) \frac{\partial R_y}{\partial t_y} \frac{\partial t_y}{\partial t_x}$$

$$\text{if } \frac{\partial t_y}{\partial t_x} = -1 \quad MR_x^* = \mu MR_x - (1 - \mu) MR_y$$

$$\frac{\partial R_y^*}{\partial t_y} = \mu \frac{\partial R_y}{\partial t_y} + (1 - \mu) \frac{\partial R_x}{\partial t_x} \frac{\partial t_x}{\partial t_y}$$

$$\text{if } \frac{\partial t_x}{\partial t_y} = -1 \quad MR_y^* = \mu MR_y - (1 - \mu) MR_x$$

The switch from a positive sign to a negative sign by taking the first derivative is due to the fact that, given the constant supply of talent, one talent more in one team implies one talent less in the other team. If the new market equilibrium is found where $MR_x^* = c_\pi^* = MR_y^*$, it can easily be derived that if $MR_x^* = MR_y^*$ then $MR_x = MR_y$. It follows that revenue sharing does not change the distribution of talent or the competitive balance in the league. It can also be shown that revenue sharing lowers the market clearing salary level:

$$c_\pi^* = MR_x^* = \mu MR_x - (1 - \mu)MR_y = \mu c_\pi - (1 - \mu)c_\pi = (2\mu - 1)c_\pi.$$

Because $2\mu - 1 < 1$, the after-sharing unit cost of talent will be lower. The reason is clear: both teams reduce their demand for talent because they have to share the additional revenue from hiring an extra talent with the opponent team. So, given the constant supply of talent, the equilibrium salary level comes down.

This result is illustrated graphically in Figure 6.1, where the player market equilibrium before and after sharing is presented. The sharing arrangement reduces the marginal revenue of both clubs by the same amount at the initial equilibrium point, which comes down to a parallel shift if the demand functions are drawn as linear curves. The dotted lines are the demand curves after sharing, and the new equilibrium is given by the point of intersection E_π^*. Compared with equilibrium E_π before sharing, one can see that the distribution of playing talent between both clubs is the same. The after-sharing salary level, however, is lower.

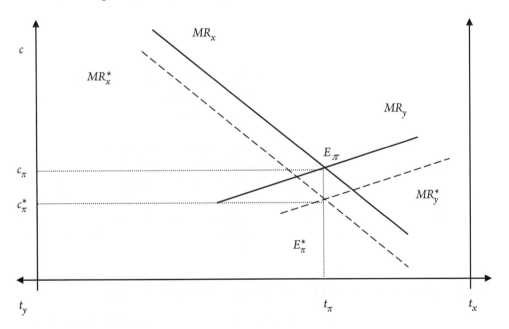

Figure 6.1 Revenue sharing under profit maximisation

In the special case of equal sharing ($\mu = 0.5$), the new market clearing salary level will be zero. If a team has to give 50 per cent of the revenue from a newly hired talent to the other team, it is no longer willing to pay for talent. A negative side-effect of this sharing arrangement is that the investment in talent is discouraged, which might reduce the absolute quality of the league.

A pool sharing system with only two teams y in the league, where both teams contribute a percentage $(1 - \omega)$ to the pool, and where the money in the pool is equally distributed, can be modelled as:

$$R_x^* = \omega R_x + \frac{(1 - \omega)}{2}(R_x + R_y)$$

$$R_y^* = \omega R_y + \frac{(1 - \omega)}{2}(R_x + R_y)$$

or

$$R_x^* = \frac{(1 + \omega)}{2} R_x + \frac{(1 - \omega)}{2} R_y$$

$$R_y^* = \frac{(1 + \omega)}{2} R_y + \frac{(1 - \omega)}{2} R_x$$

This pool sharing system turns out to be the same as the gate sharing system (6.1), with:

$$\mu = \frac{1 + \omega}{2} \quad \text{and} \quad (1 - \mu) = \frac{1 - \omega}{2}.$$

It is important, though, to remark here that all results, based on a two-team model, are not necessarily true for a more general n-club model. The case of a more general n-team model is dealt with in the appendix to this chapter.

Another interesting question is how revenue sharing affects the profits of the team owners. As shown in the appendix, for an n-team model, revenue sharing increases the profits of the small and the mid-sized teams. Only for teams that have a pre-sharing profit that is higher than the average team budget in the league does revenue sharing lower profits. But revenue sharing increases league-wide profits. These results are independent of the size of the share parameter (see Késenne, 2007a).

6.2.2 Revenue sharing in a win-maximisation league

The impact of revenue sharing in a league where all the teams are win maximisers is totally different from that in a profit-maximisation league. As seen in

Chapter 3, the demand curves for talent in a win-maximisation league, with zero capital cost and zero profits, are determined by the AR revenue curves. With a gate sharing system (6.1), which is equivalent to a pool sharing system with only two clubs, we can derive that:

$$R_x^* = \mu R_x + (1 - \mu)R_y < R_x$$

$$R_y^* = \mu R_y + (1 - \mu)R_x > R_y$$

and so

$$AR_x^* = R_x^*/t_x < R_x/t_x = AR_x$$

$$AR_y^* > AR_y$$

It follows that the large-market team x will reduce its demand for talent and the small-market team y will increase its demand for talent, resulting in an improved competitive balance. One can also derive that the unit cost of talent, or the average player salary level, will increase. Assume that, after sharing, 1000 euros have been transferred from the large team x to the small team y. It follows that the demand of the large team, being the average revenue curve, decreases with $\frac{1000}{t_x}$ and the small team's demand curve increases with $\frac{1000}{t_y}$. Because $t_x > t_y$, the downward shift of the large team's demand curve will be smaller than the upward shift of the small team's demand curve, causing an increase in the salary level. This is shown in Figure 6.2.

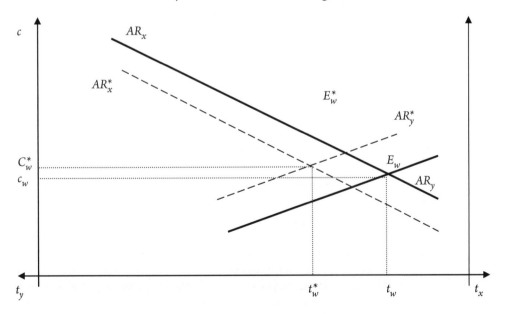

Figure 6.2 Revenue sharing under win maximisation

After revenue sharing the large-market club's demand curve for talent has shifted downwards, whereas the small-market club's demand curve has shifted upwards, so the new market equilibrium results in a more balanced distribution of playing talent. But, because the size of the shifts of the demand curves is different for both clubs, the after-sharing salary level will be higher.

Again, the results for an n-team league are presented in the appendix to this chapter.

6.3 Revenue sharing in the Nash equilibrium model

Earlier studies dealing with the impact of revenue sharing always started from the Walras model and the assumption that the supply of talent is fixed (see Fort and Quirk, 1995). Moreover, they also assumed that team owners take this fixed talent supply into account in their hiring decisions. Team owners know that one extra talent not only strengthens their own team, but also weakens the opponent team in the league. If owners internalise the negative externality of talent hiring on the other team, the demand for talent of one team is not affected by the hiring strategies of the other team. It follows that owners can choose the winning percentage of their team, which is not a very realistic property of this model.

If the supply of talent is flexible, as discussed in Chapter 3, a Nash equilibrium model applies. The game that is considered is again a non-cooperative game with an exogenously given marginal cost of talent where all teams decide on the hiring of talents, taking into account the talent hiring of their opponents in the league.

6.3.1 Revenue sharing and profit maximisation

As distinct from the previous result, it can be shown that in a two-club Nash equilibrium model revenue sharing worsens the competitive balance under the **profit-maximisation** hypothesis (see Szymanski, 2003, 2004; Szymanski and Késenne, 2004). This can be explained by the fact that revenue sharing partly neutralises the negative external effects that teams have on each other when hiring talent, because revenue sharing lowers the marginal revenue of talent. Given that the large-market team has a higher marginal revenue of talent, the negative external effect that the small-market team has on the large-market club is larger than the external effect that the large-market team has on the small-market club, so the small-market team is worse off if these externalities are partly neutralised.

This can be shown using a model with very simplified revenue functions. Assume that the revenue function of the large-market team is $R_x = \alpha w_x$ with $\alpha = m_x / m_y > 1$, and the revenue function of the small-market club is $R_y = w_y$. These revenue functions are linear in win percentage, but concave in talent, because $w_x = \frac{t_x}{t_x + t_y}$ and $w_y = \frac{t_y}{t_x + t_y}$. With a constant marginal cost of talent, the Nash equilibrium can then be found at the point of intersection of the reaction curves, that is, $\frac{\alpha t_y}{(t_x + t_y)^2} = \frac{t_x}{(t_x + t_y)^2}$, so the competitive balance is $\frac{t_x}{t_y} = \alpha > 1$. The large-market club is more talented than the small-market club. If revenues are shared, with a star indicating the after-sharing values, revenues are:

$$R_x^* = \mu\alpha w_x + (1 - \mu)w_y$$

$$R_y^* = \mu w_y + (1 - \mu)\alpha w_x.$$

The new Nash equilibrium is then found where:

$$\frac{\partial R_x^*}{\partial t_x} = \frac{\mu\alpha t_y - (1 - \mu)t_y}{(t_x + t_y)^2} = \frac{\partial R_y^*}{\partial t_y} = \frac{\mu t_x - (1 - \mu)\alpha t_x}{(t_x + t_y)^2}.$$

The competitive balance $\frac{t_x^*}{t_y^*} = \frac{\mu\alpha + \mu - 1}{\mu\alpha + \mu - \alpha} > \alpha$ indicates that revenue sharing worsens the competitive balance (see Szymanski, 2003; Szymanski and Késenne, 2004).

Another implication of revenue sharing in this Nash equilibrium model is that, with a given salary level, the number of talents hired by each club decreases. This can be seen by comparing the demand for talent, or the marginal revenue, before and after sharing.

Because $\mu\alpha - (1 - \mu) < \alpha$ and $\mu - (1 - \mu)\alpha < 1$, it follows that the league is less talented, so the absolute quality of play diminishes, which can have a negative effect on attendances, gate receipts and other club revenues.

Dietl and Lang (2008) have analysed the effect of gate revenue on social welfare, starting from a general fan utility function, and concluded that revenue sharing worsens the competitive balance but improves social welfare in a Nash equilibrium model.

A prize fund as an alternative sharing system

An alternative sharing system consists of the creation of a prize fund. So far, we have assumed that the contribution of each club to the pool is linked to the size of its budget and that the money is redistributed equally, and not linked to any performance indicator such as the winning percentage, the TV coverage or the quality of youth training. Using a simplified model, Szymanski (2003) has investigated the impact of a sharing system where each team has to contribute a fixed amount to a prize fund that is redistributed according to the winning percentage of the team. If the revenue function of the large-market team is again $R_x = \alpha w_x$ with $\alpha > 1$ and that of the small-market club is $R_y = w_y$, we have seen that the Nash equilibrium yields the competitive balance: $\frac{t_x}{t_y} = \alpha$. Assume that a fund v is created with an equal contribution $v/2$ by both teams. Each club receives a share of that fund according to its winning percentage, that is, $w_x v$ and $w_y v$. If a star again indicates the after-sharing values, we find that:

$$R_x^* = \alpha w_x - v/2 + w_x v$$

$$R_y^* = w_y - v/2 + w_y v.$$

The Nash equilibrium can then be found at the point of intersection of the reaction functions $\frac{(\alpha + v)t_y}{(t_x + t_y)^2} = c = \frac{(1 + v)t_x}{(t_x + t_y)^2}$, so the after-sharing competitive balance is $\frac{t_x^*}{t_y^*} = \frac{\alpha + v}{1 + v} < \alpha$.

Using a very simple model, it is shown that this specific revenue-sharing arrangement improves the competitive balance.

6.3.2 Revenue sharing and win maximisation

Under the win-maximisation hypothesis, the Nash equilibrium is the same as the Walras equilibrium, as seen in Chapter 3. It is obvious that, if teams are win maximisers who spend their whole budget on talent, revenue sharing will also improve the competitive balance, as it did in the Walras model in section 6.2. Under win maximisation, the reaction functions, after sharing, can be written simply as:

$$AR_x^* = c = AR_y^*.$$

Because revenue sharing increases the total and the average revenue of the small-market team, it will increase its demand for talent. The large-market club will decrease its demand for talent, so the result is an improved competitive balance.

Market-size-based sharing?

It is possible that a well-managed small-market team could dominate a poorly managed large-market team. In this rather exceptional case, revenue sharing might have a possibly unwanted effect on the distribution of talent in a win-maximisation league. The revenue-sharing system above will still improve the competitive balance, but in this case the ill-performing large-market club profits from the sharing arrangement to the disadvantage of the well-performing small-market club. The reason is that the small-market club also has the larger budget if it is more talented than the large-market club. Therefore, one might consider a sharing system that is not based on the size of the budget, but on the size of the market. The following sharing arrangement can serve as an example:

$$R_i^* = R_i - \frac{1}{\mu}(m_i - \overline{m}) \quad \text{with} \quad \mu > 0,$$

where $\overline{m}$ is the average market size in the league. Again, a higher value of the parameter μ means less sharing. This sharing arrangement implies a money transfer from the large-market team to the small-market team and not from the high-budget team to the low-budget team. This arrangement not only has the advantage of establishing a more balanced competition, but also avoids the disadvantage that the small-market team is punished for performing better than the large-market team. Moreover, this sharing arrangement increases total league revenue, because it moves the win-maximisation equilibrium closer to the profit-maximisation equilibrium.

In a profit-maximisation league, this sharing arrangement would not change the competitive balance, because the teams' marginal revenues are not affected.

6.4   Conclusion

The case for revenue sharing in a **profit-maximisation** league is not very strong. In the benchmark scenario of Rottenberg (1956), Quirk and El-Hodiri (1974) and Quirk and Fort (1992), the so-called invariance proposition, stating that revenue sharing does not affect the competitive balance, holds. Moreover, the allocation of talent is optimal in terms of league-wide revenue if clubs are profit maximisers, so revenue sharing, which leads to a less efficient allocation of talent, is not called for. So far, to the best of our knowledge, the impact of revenue sharing in the most realistic scenario has not been analysed. This scenario should include a league with more than two teams, where team revenue is affected both by the winning percentage of the home and the visiting teams, and by the absolute quality, where the revenue-sharing arrangement includes the sharing of gate receipts, the pool sharing of broadcasting rights and the non-sharing of other revenue, and where the talent supply can be fixed or flexible, and analysed using the appropriate model. Some partial results show that revenue sharing can improve or worsen the competitive balance, which leads to the general conclusion that the impact of revenue sharing on the competitive balance can expected to be rather limited in the profit-maximisation scenario (see also Feess and Stähler, 2009).

Applied to the North American major leagues, where clubs are assumed to be profit maximisers, revenue sharing will not have a strong effect on competitive balance.

In the national soccer leagues in Europe, where teams are assumed to behave like win or utility maximisers, revenue sharing is effective in establishing a more balanced distribution of talent. After the abolition of the transfer system by the Bosman verdict, revenue sharing became even more appropriate, because the small-market teams, being net sellers of talent on the transfer market, lost some revenue.

An interesting feature of revenue sharing is that whatever the model one starts from – Walras or Nash equilibrium, profit or win maximisation – revenue sharing improves the allocation of talent in terms of maximising league-wide revenue. However, a more efficient allocation of talent does not always imply a more equal distribution of talent. In the Nash equilibrium model under profit maximisation, revenue sharing improves the allocation of talent but worsens the competitive balance. The pre-sharing distribution of talent in a Walras model league under win maximisation is more unequal than under profit maximisation, and so the allocation of talent is inefficient; too many talents are playing in the large-market team. So revenue sharing improves both the competitive balance and the allocation of talent.

? **EXERCISES 6**

6.1 If in a two-club league with revenue functions:

$$R_x = 12t_x - 6t_x^2 \qquad \text{and} \qquad R_y = 8t_y - 4t_y^2$$

the share parameter in the gate sharing arrangement is $\mu = 0.8$, derive the distribution of talent and the equilibrium salary level if both clubs are profit maximisers. (Before sharing, $t_x^\pi = 0.6$, $t_y^\pi = 0.4$ and $c^\pi = 4.8$.)

6.2 Assuming the following club revenue functions:

$$R_x = 200t_x - 100t_x^2 \qquad \text{and} \qquad R_y = 80t_y - 100t_y^2$$

and only player costs, derive the clubs' revenues, the average league revenue, the clubs' profits and total league profits for the following share parameter values in a pool sharing system: $\mu = 1, 0.5$ and 0. What do you conclude concerning the impact of revenue sharing on profits?

6.3 Let the revenue functions of the large- and the small-market clubs again be given by:

$$R_x = 160t_x - 100\,t_x^2 \qquad \text{and} \qquad R_y = 120t_y - 100t_y^2.$$

Without sharing, the distribution of talent is $t_x^w / t_y^w = 0.7/0.3$ under win maximisation and $t_x^\pi / t_y^\pi = 0.6/0.4$ under profit maximisation. Assume now that the following sharing arrangement is imposed:

$$R_i^* = R_i - \frac{t_i}{\mu}(m_i - \overline{m}) \qquad \text{with} \qquad \mu = 2.$$

How does this sharing system affect the distribution of talent in a win-maximisation league?

Appendix

Revenue sharing in an n-team league

In this appendix, we consider the impact of revenue sharing in the case of a more general n-team league. Because gate sharing and pool sharing are not equivalent in an n-team model, we analyse both scenarios in a profit- and in a win-maximisation league.

6A.1   Pool sharing in a Walras model under profit maximisation

We start with the impact of redistributing the clubs' season revenue in a pool sharing system with a fixed-share parameter. It implies that all clubs in a league have to contribute a fixed percentage of their season revenue to a pool or a fund, administered by the league authorities, and that the money is redistributed equally among all clubs:

$$R_i^* = \mu R_i + \frac{(1 - \mu)}{n} \sum_{j=1}^{n} R_j = \mu R_i + (1 - \mu)\bar{R} \quad \text{with} \ 0 \leq \mu < 1, \tag{6A.1}$$

where $\bar{R}$ is the average revenue in the league and μ is the share parameter. A higher value of the share parameter means less sharing; a value of zero means equal sharing.

In order to investigate the impact of revenue sharing on the distribution of talent, we look at the partial derivatives of the clubs' demand curves for talent with respect to the share parameter (see Marburger, 1997a). This methodology is based on the reasonable assumption that the competitive balance improves (worsens) if the downward shift of the demand curves for talent of the large-market clubs is larger (smaller) than the downward shift of the demand curves for talent of the small-market clubs. So, we need to compare the partial derivatives of the clubs' demand curves after sharing with respect to the share parameter at the initial market equilibrium point.

If clubs are profit maximisers, the demand curves for talent after sharing are the marginal revenue curves after sharing:

$$\frac{\partial R_i^*}{\partial t_i} = \mu \frac{\partial R_i}{\partial t_i} + \frac{(1 - \mu)}{n} \sum_{j=1}^{n} \frac{\partial R_j}{\partial t_j} \frac{\partial t_j}{\partial t_i}.$$

Given the constant supply of talent in the Walras model, one more talent for team i implies a loss of one talent in another team, say team k, so $\frac{\partial t_k}{\partial t_i} = -1$ and:

$$\frac{\partial R_i^*}{\partial t_i} = \mu \frac{\partial R_i}{\partial t_i} + \frac{(1-\mu)}{n} \frac{\partial R_i}{\partial t_i} - \frac{(1-\mu)}{n} \frac{\partial R_k}{\partial t_k}. \qquad (6A.2)$$

After taking the partial derivative of these demand curves with respect to μ, we find that:

$$\frac{\partial(\partial R_i^*/\partial t_i)}{\partial \mu} = \frac{\partial R_i}{\partial t_i} - \frac{1}{n}\frac{\partial R_i}{\partial t_i} + \frac{1}{n}\frac{\partial R_k}{\partial t_k}.$$

Because we have to compare the shifts of the demand curves at the profit-maximising equilibrium point where, in a competitive market, each team's marginal revenue equals the market clearing unit cost of talent, we can write that:

$$\frac{\partial(\partial R_i^*/\partial t_i)}{\partial \mu} = c_\pi\left(1 - \frac{1}{n} + \frac{1}{n}\right) = c_\pi. \qquad (6A.3)$$

Because these partial derivatives are clearly positive, revenue sharing causes a decrease in the demand for talent of all clubs. As a consequence, the unit cost of talent, or the average player salary, will also come down. The new market clearing salary level can be derived as follows, using (6A.2):

$$c_\pi^* = \frac{\partial R_i^*}{\partial t_i} = c_\pi\left(\mu + \frac{(1-\mu)}{n} - \frac{(1-\mu)}{n}\right) = \mu c_\pi.$$

A more important result from this analysis is that the distribution of talent, or the competitive balance in the league, is not affected by pool revenue sharing. As can be seen from (6A.3), the shift in the demand for talent is the same in each club. All clubs equally reduce their demand for talent, because they all have to share the revenue from an extra talent with the other clubs. This result holds regardless of the specification of the revenue function and confirms Rottenberg's (1956) invariance proposition that revenue sharing does not affect the competitive balance in a profit-maximisation league.

6A.2 Gate sharing in a Walras model under profit maximisation

Another way to share revenue, although rather unknown in European professional sports, is the sharing of gate receipts. American football in the National Football League (NFL) presents the best example of this arrangement. Besides the equal sharing of national broadcast rights, the NFL home teams can keep only 60 per cent of their ticket sales; 40 per cent goes to the visiting team.

Assuming that in a championship each team plays one home and one away game against every other team, the number of games played by each team is

$2(n-1)$. The revenue of club i, playing a home game against club j, is represented by R_{ij}. If the share parameter is again represented by μ, the total season revenue of each club, after sharing, can be written as:

$$R_i^* = \mu \sum_{j \neq i}^{n} R_{ij} + (1 - \mu) \sum_{j \neq i}^{n} R_{ji} \quad \text{with} \quad 0.5 \leq \mu < 1 \quad \text{for all } i. \tag{6A.4}$$

For individual games, club revenue is affected not only by the size of the market and its own winning percentage, but also by the quality of the visiting team, which can be represented by the winning percentage of the visiting team. Spectators prefer to watch two high-quality teams playing rather than two poor teams, whatever the closeness of the game or the championship. Marburger (1997a), in his analysis of revenue sharing, used the number of playing talents in both teams as an approximation of the absolute quality of the play. Referring to the ticket demand function, as specified in Chapter 2, we will use the following revenue function, which includes, in a constant supply Walras equilibrium approach, the talents of the visiting team:

$$R_{ij} = R_{ij}(m_i, t_i, t_j) \quad \text{for all } i, j, \tag{6A.5}$$

where the usual assumptions hold that:

$$\frac{\partial R_{ij}}{\partial m_i} > 0 \quad \frac{\partial R_{ij}}{\partial t_i} > 0 \quad \frac{\partial R_{ij}}{\partial t_i} > 0 \quad \frac{\partial^2 R_{ij}}{\partial t_i^2} < 0.$$

We also assume that the impact of a team's talents on its home game attendance is larger than on the away game attendance:

$$\frac{\partial R_{ij}}{\partial t_i} > \frac{\partial R_{ji}}{\partial t_i} \quad \text{and} \quad \frac{\partial R_{ji}}{\partial t_j} > \frac{\partial R_{ij}}{\partial t_j}. \tag{6A.6}$$

The demand curves for talent on a competitive player labour market under the profit-maximisation assumption are then given by:

$$\frac{\partial R_i^*}{\partial t_i} = \mu \sum_{j \neq i}^{n} \frac{\partial R_{ij}}{\partial t_i} + (1 - \mu) \sum_{j \neq i}^{n} \frac{\partial R_{ji}}{\partial t_i} \quad \text{for all } i.$$

Because the supply of talent is constant, a talent increase in one team implies a loss of talent in at least one other team, or, if the loss is symmetrically spread over all other teams, the change in talent of these clubs is:

$$\frac{\partial t_j}{\partial t_i} = \frac{-1}{n - 1} \quad \text{for all } i \neq j.$$

How does revenue sharing, or a decrease in the share parameter μ, affect the distribution of playing talent? We will again consider the shifts in the demand curves for talent of the large- and the small-market clubs. These shifts are given by the first derivatives of the marginal revenue functions with respect to the share parameter μ:

$$\frac{\partial(\partial R_i^*/\partial t_i)}{\partial \mu} = \sum_{j \neq i}^{n} \left\{ \frac{\partial R_{ij}}{\partial t_i} - \frac{\partial R_{ji}}{\partial t_i} + \frac{1}{n-1}\left(\frac{\partial R_{ji}}{\partial t_j} - \frac{\partial R_{ij}}{\partial t_j} \right) \right\}. \quad (6A.7)$$

Based on the assumptions made in (6A.5), the sign of the right-hand side of (6A.7) is positive, so the demand for playing talent of each club will be reduced. As a consequence, the market clearing player salary level will come down.

What is the impact of gate sharing on the talent distribution? This can be derived again by comparing the shifts in talent demand of the large- and the small-market clubs at the initial market equilibrium point. If the size of the shifts is the same for all clubs, that is, independent of i, gate sharing does not affect the distribution of talent.

Unfortunately, this cannot be seen from (6A.7), which is based on the general concave revenue function (6A.5). A simple counter-example, however, using a quadratic revenue function, shows that revenue sharing can have a positive impact on the talent distribution. Let the revenue function be specified as:

$$R_{ij} = m_i t_i - 0.5 t_i^2 + \gamma_i t_j, \quad (6A.8)$$

where the parameter ε_i captures the positive impact of the quality of the visiting team. We assume that its value depends only on the size of the market of club i: the larger the drawing potential of a club, the higher the value of γ_i. Given this revenue function, expression (6A.7) can now be derived to be:

$$\frac{\partial(\partial R_i^*/\partial t_i)}{\partial \mu} = \frac{n(n-2)}{(n-1)}(m_i - t_i) + \frac{n}{(n-1)}[\bar{m} - \bar{t} - (n-1)\bar{\gamma}], \quad (6A.9)$$

where $\bar{m}$, $\bar{t}$ and $\bar{\gamma}$ are the average values of m_i, t_i and γ_i.

In the labour market equilibrium without revenue sharing, it holds for all clubs that:

$$\frac{\partial R_i^*}{\partial t_i} = \sum_{i \neq j}^{n} \frac{\partial R_{ij}}{\partial t_i} = c_\pi, \quad \text{so} \quad (n-1)(m_i - t_i) - \gamma_i = c_\pi. \quad (6A.10)$$

Substituting (6A.10) into (6A.9) yields:

$$\frac{\partial(\partial R_i^*/\partial t_i)}{\partial \mu} = \frac{n(n-2)}{(n-1)^2}(c_\pi + \gamma_i) + \frac{n}{(n-1)}[\bar{m} - \bar{t} - (n-1)\bar{\gamma}].$$

(6A.11)

From this result, one can see that the shifts in the demand curves for talent, caused by gate sharing, are different for every club. The higher the value of the parameter ε_i, the larger will be the downward shift in labour demand. Because γ_i is larger for the large-market clubs, they will reduce their demand for playing talent more than the small-market clubs. It follows that the new market equilibrium after sharing shows a more equal distribution of talent, yielding a more balanced competition if clubs are profit maximisers.

Remarks

1. From equation (6A.11) it can be seen that gate sharing has no impact on the distribution of talent if $\gamma_i = 0$, that is, if the winning percentage, or the talents, of the visiting team does not appear in the revenue function, or if $\gamma_i = \gamma$ for all i, that is, if the impact of the visiting team's quality on revenue is the same for every club. In both cases, the downward shifts of the demand curves are the same for every club. Also, if the values of γ_i are small or the differences between the values of γ_i are small, gate sharing will be quite ineffective in changing the competitive balance in a league.
2. Expression (6A.11) also indicates that, if there are only two teams in a league ($n = 2$), gate sharing has no impact on the distribution of talent even if the parameter ε_i is different for every club. It follows that the results from a two-club model do not generally apply to a more general n-club model. Also notice that, apart from the value of the share parameter, this gate sharing arrangement and the pool sharing arrangement of the previous section are the same if there are only two clubs in the league.
3. What if a club also receives revenues that are not shared, such as local broadcasting rights in some US major leagues? From the counter-example above, it can be seen that in this case the conclusion of Fort and Quirk (1995) holds that gate sharing changes the competitive balance. If R_{ij}^0 indicates the non-shared revenues, the after-sharing revenue of each club in (6A.4) has be adjusted to:

$$R_i^* = \mu \sum_{j \neq i}^n R_{ij} + (1 - \mu) \sum_{j \neq i}^n R_{ji} + \sum_{j \neq i}^n R_{ij}^0.$$

If the impact of t_i on the non-shared revenues is assumed to be r_i, (6A.11) becomes:

$$\frac{\partial(\partial R_i^*/\partial t_i)}{\partial\mu} = \frac{n(n-2)}{(n-1)^2}(c_\pi + \gamma_i - (n-1)r_i) + \frac{n}{(n-1)}$$

$$(\overline{m} - \overline{t} - (n-1)\overline{\gamma}).$$

This shows that the downward shift of the demand curve also depends on the different impact of talent on local TV rights: the larger r_i, the smaller the downward shift of the demand curve. If $\gamma_i = 0$, as Fort and Quirk (1995) assume, and r_i is larger for the large-market clubs, revenue sharing will yield a more unequal distribution of talent. If not, the outcome is theoretically indeterminate, because the sign of $\gamma_i - (n-1)r_i$ is unknown.

6A.3   Pool sharing in a Walras model under win maximisation

Knowing that the demand for playing talent of the win-maximising club is given by its net average revenue (NAR) curve, the clubs' demand curves after sharing are given by:

$$NAR_i^* = \frac{1}{t_i}(\mu R_i + (1-\mu)\overline{R} - c_i^0).$$

Taking the partial derivative with respect to the share parameter yields:

$$\frac{\partial NAR_i^*}{\partial\mu} = \frac{1}{t_i}(R_i - \overline{R}). \tag{6A.12}$$

Because the right-hand side of this equation is clearly positive for a large-budget club, its demand curve for playing talent shifts downwards if the degree of revenue sharing increases. For a small-budget club, the demand curve for playing talent shifts upwards. A club with a budget that is exactly equal to the average budget in the league will not change its demand for talent. It follows that this revenue-sharing arrangement improves the distribution of playing talent in a win-maximisation league. This result holds regardless of the specification of the revenue function and the size of the capital cost.

In order to find out how revenue sharing affects the salary level, we have to compare the size of the shifts of the large- and the small-budget clubs at the market equilibrium point where $NAR_i = c_w$ for all i.

If the non-labour cost is again assumed to be proportional to the club's budget: $c_i^0 = kR_i$, so $NAR_i = (1-k)AR_i$, we can derive from (6A.12) that:

$$\frac{\partial NAR_i^*}{\partial \mu} = \frac{NAR_i}{1-k} - \frac{\bar{R}}{t_i} = \frac{c_w}{1-k} - \frac{\bar{R}}{t_i}.$$

It follows that the downward shift of the demand curves of the talented large-budget clubs are smaller than the upward shift of the demand curves of less talented small-budget clubs, so the equilibrium salary level goes up.

This result can also be explained by considering that revenue sharing moves the labour market equilibrium in a win-maximisation league closer to the profit-maximisation equilibrium where total league revenue is at its maximum level, as has been derived in Chapter 3. Because the salary level in the win-maximisation equilibrium is equal to the ratio of total league net revenue and the constant and normalised $(s = n/2)$ supply of playing talent, that is, $c_w = \frac{2(1-k)}{n} \sum_{j=1}^{n} R_j$, it follows that the salary reaches its highest level when total league revenue is at its highest level. However, with a very low value of the share parameter, which means a very high degree of sharing, the outcome can be a more equal distribution of talent than in the profit-maximisation equilibrium, so the salary level will come down again.

6A.4 Gate sharing in a Walras model under win maximisation

If the demand for talent under win maximisation is given by the net average revenue curve, and if gate revenues are shared according to sharing arrangement (6A.4), the demand for talent after sharing can be written as:

$$NAR_i^* = \frac{1}{t_i}\left(\mu \sum_{j \neq i}^{n} R_{ij} + (1-\mu) \sum_{j \neq i}^{n} R_{ji}\right) - \frac{c_i^0}{t_i}.$$

Taking the first-order derivative with respect to μ yields:

$$\frac{\partial NAR_i^*}{\partial \mu} = \frac{1}{t_i}\left(\sum_{j \neq i}^{n} R_{ij} - \sum_{j \neq i}^{n} R_{ji}\right). \tag{6A.13}$$

The sign of this derivative indicates again the direction of the shift in the demand curves for talent. For large-market clubs, (6A.13) is positive, because $R_{ij} > R_{ji}$. For small-market clubs, (6A.13) is negative. It follows that large-market clubs will lower their talent demand and small-market clubs will increase their demand for talent. The result is a more equal distribution of playing talent and a more balanced league championship. It is also important to mention that a high- or a low-capital cost or profit rate does not change the conclusion that revenue sharing improves the competitive balance. If large-market clubs are interested in a higher profit rate, they will spend less money on playing talent and contribute to a more equal distribution of playing talent in this way.

The impact of gate sharing on the salary level in a win maximisation league is the same as the impact of pool sharing. Initially the unit cost of talent, and the average player salary, goes up, because sharing moves the distribution of talent closer to the Pareto-optimal profit-maximisation equilibrium, but, once the league revenue-maximising distribution of talent is reached, further revenue sharing will lower the salary level.

Remarks

1. It is possible that, in the win-maximisation equilibrium before sharing, the marginal revenue of the large-market team is negative. Its winning percentage can be so high that, because of a lack of uncertainty of outcome, public interest fades and total season revenue decreases. In that case, revenue sharing can increase not only the season revenue of the small-market team, but also the season revenue of the large-market team if the increase in revenue, owing to more intense competition, outbalances the negative effect on its revenue (see Késenne, 1996).
2. It is also worth considering the Rascher (1997) utility-maximisation model, which assumes that clubs maximise a linear combination of profit and wins (or talent), given by the following function:

$$u_i = \pi_i + \alpha_i t_i = (R_i - ct_i - c_i^0) + \alpha_i t_i \qquad \text{with } a_i > 0.$$

If $a_i > 1$, more weight is put on wins. The impact of the share parameter μ on the demand for playing talent in this model is the same as the right-hand side of (6A.7). This indicates again that revenue sharing causes a reduction in the demand for talent by all clubs and a decrease in the salary level. However, contrary to the case for the profit-maximisation model, the reduction of playing talent is not the same in every club. If clubs put different weights on winning, revenue sharing changes the distribution of playing talent. This can be shown again by the counter-example. Given revenue function (6A.8), expression (6A.11) becomes:

$$\frac{n(n-2)}{(n-1)^2}(c_{\pi w} + \gamma_i - \alpha_i) + \frac{n}{(n-1)}[\bar{m} - \bar{t} - (n-1)\bar{\gamma}].$$

If there are only two clubs in the league, revenue sharing has no impact on the distribution of playing talent. But if $n > 2$ the first term indicates that the reaction of each club to revenue sharing also depends on the weight it puts on winning α_i. It turns out that a club that shows a greater interest in profit making will reduce its demand for playing talent more than a club that is more win orientated. The conclusion is that, under the reasonable assumption that large-market clubs care more about profits, revenue sharing causes a stronger downward shift in their demand for talent, so revenue sharing has a positive impact on the distribution of playing talent. The same result can be found for a pool sharing system.

6A.5   Revenue sharing and owners' profits

An interesting question is how revenue sharing affects the profits of a club. Revenue sharing obviously increases the profits of the low-budget clubs, as well as total league profits. It is less clear, however, how the profits of the large-budget clubs are affected. Revenue sharing lowers the large-budget clubs' revenue, but, as has been shown above, the player labour cost is also expected to come down. In this section we will analyse the impact on profits of a pool sharing system as specified in (6A.1).

Assuming that club managers are well informed about the sharing arrangement, they will take it into account in their hiring decisions. Because revenue sharing affects talent demand and unit cost of talent, both club revenue and cost are affected. If a club's season profit is the difference between season revenue and season cost, the after-sharing profit function can be written as:

$$\pi_i^* = \mu R_i[m, t_i^*] + (1 - \mu)\overline{R}[m, t^*] - c^* t_i^* - c_i^0,$$

where the stars indicate the after-sharing values and m and t are n-vectors of the market sizes and talents. In order to analyse the impact of revenue sharing on profits, the partial derivative of the profit function with respect to μ is calculated:

$$\frac{\partial \pi_i^*}{\partial \mu} = R_i[m, t_i^*] - \overline{R}[m, t^*] + \frac{\partial \overline{R}[m, t^*]}{\partial \mu}$$

$$+ \mu\left(\frac{\partial R_i[m, t_i^*]}{\partial \mu} - \frac{\partial \overline{R}[m, t^*]}{\partial \mu}\right) - c^* \frac{\partial t_i^*}{\partial \mu} - t_i^* \frac{\partial c^*}{\partial \mu}. \quad (6A.14)$$

A positive sign for this equation means that more revenue sharing will lower club profits.

As analysed above, revenue sharing leaves the talent distribution unchanged and lowers the competitive salary level. It follows that (6A.14) simplifies to:

$$\frac{\partial \pi_i^*}{\partial \mu} = R_i[m_i, t_i] - \bar{R}[m, t] - t_i \frac{\partial c^*}{\partial \mu} = R_i[m_i, t_i] - \bar{R}[m, t] - ct_i = \pi_i - \bar{R},$$
(6A.15)

where c is the market clearing unit cost of talent before sharing. As has been shown before, the equilibrium unit cost of talent after sharing is $c^* = \mu c$, so $\frac{\partial c^*}{\partial \mu} = c$.

Because the right-hand side of equation (6A.15) is clearly negative for all clubs that have a pre-sharing budget that is smaller than or equal to the average budget in the league, revenue sharing increases the profits of the small and mid-sized clubs. Only for teams that have budgets that are so large, compared with those of the other teams in the league, that their pre-sharing profits are higher than the average budget in the league will revenue sharing lower profits. Also notice that the size of the share parameter μ does not affect this result. Even the most modest sharing arrangement can lower the profits of the very dominant clubs.

The positive impact of revenue sharing on league-wide profits can also be easily derived. Total league profits after sharing can be written as:

$$\sum_{i=1}^{n} \pi_i^* = \sum_{i=1}^{n} R_i[m_i, t_i^*] - \sum_{i=1}^{n} (c^* t_i^* + c_i^0).$$

Because sharing does not change the talent distribution and the supply of talent is constant, its impact on league-wide profits can be found as:

$$\frac{\partial \sum_{i=1}^{n} \pi_i^*}{\partial \mu} = -\sum_{i=1}^{n} ct_i^* = -cs < 0.$$

Because total league revenue is not altered and the total player cost is coming down, revenue sharing increases total league profits (see Késenne, 2007a).

6A.6 *Revenue sharing in a Nash model under profit maximisation*

It can be shown that the result, that revenue sharing worsens the competitive balance, also holds for an n-club model with more general revenue functions (see Késenne, 2005). To show this, let's start from the pool sharing system in (6A.1), which is repeated here:

$$R_i^* = \mu R_i + \frac{(1 - \mu)}{n} \sum_{j=1}^{n} R_j = \mu R_i + (1 - \mu)\bar{R}.$$

To find the impact of this sharing system on the distribution of talent, we will investigate again the shifts of the teams' demand curves for talent. The assumption is that revenue sharing worsens the competitive balance if, for any pair of clubs in the league, the downward shift of the demand curve of the high-talented club is smaller than the downward shift of the demand curve of the low-talented club at the initial player market equilibrium point.

If a club is a profit maximiser, its demand curve for talent is given by the marginal revenue:

$$\frac{\partial R_i^*}{\partial t_i} = \mu \frac{\partial R_i}{\partial t_i} + \frac{(1-\mu)}{n} \frac{\partial R_i}{\partial t_i} + \frac{(1-\mu)}{n} \sum_{j \neq i}^{n} \frac{\partial R_j}{\partial t_i}.$$

The size of the shifts of these demand curves is given by the partial derivative of this marginal revenue function with respect to the share parameter μ:

$$\frac{\partial R_i^*/\partial t_i}{\partial \mu} = \frac{(n-1)}{n} \frac{\partial R_i}{\partial t_i} - \frac{1}{n} \sum_{j \neq i}^{n} \frac{\partial R_j}{\partial t_i}. \tag{6A.16}$$

Because this expression is clearly positive, revenue sharing causes all clubs to reduce their demand for playing talent. More important is the size of these shifts at the initial equilibrium point, that is, at the point where the club's marginal revenue equals the market clearing unit cost of talent before sharing:

$$\frac{\partial R_i}{\partial t_i} = \frac{\partial R_i}{\partial w_i} \frac{\partial w_i}{\partial t_i} = c_\pi \quad \text{for all } i. \tag{6A.17}$$

By substituting (6A.17) into (6A.16) for all clubs, and given that $\frac{\partial R_j}{\partial t_i}$ can also be written as $\frac{\partial R_j}{\partial w_j} \frac{\partial w_j}{\partial t_i} \frac{\partial w_j}{\partial t_j} / \frac{\partial w_j}{\partial t_j}$, one finds that:

$$\frac{\partial R_i^*/\partial t_i}{\partial \mu} = \frac{(n-1)}{n} c_\pi - \frac{1}{n} \sum_{j \neq i}^{n} c_\pi - \frac{1}{n} \sum_{j \neq i}^{n} c_\pi \frac{\partial w_j}{\partial t_i} / \frac{\partial w_j}{\partial t_j}$$

$$= c_\pi \left\{ \frac{(n-1)}{n} + \frac{1}{n} \sum_{j \neq i}^{n} \left(\frac{t_j}{\sum_{k \neq j}^{n} t_k} \right) \right\}. \tag{6A.18}$$

From this result it can be derived that club i, with the high number of playing talents before sharing (which is in this general model not necessarily the large-market club), will reduce its demand for talent less than club k, with the low number of playing talents:

$$\text{if} \quad t_i > t_k \quad \text{then} \quad \frac{\partial R_i^*/\partial t_i}{\partial \mu} < \frac{\partial R_k^*/\partial t_k}{\partial \mu}. \tag{6A.19}$$

It follows that this revenue-sharing arrangement worsens the competitive balance.

A numerical example with only three clubs in the league can illustrate this result. For the three clubs the downward shifts of the demand curves, according to expression (6A.18), are:

club 1:
$$c\left\{\frac{2}{3} + \frac{1}{3}\left(\frac{t_2}{t_1 + t_3} + \frac{t_3}{t_1 + t_2}\right)\right\}$$

club 2:
$$c\left\{\frac{2}{3} + \frac{1}{3}\left(\frac{t_1}{t_2 + t_3} + \frac{t_3}{t_1 + t_2}\right)\right\}$$

club 3:
$$c\left\{\frac{2}{3} + \frac{1}{3}\left(\frac{t_1}{t_2 + t_3} + \frac{t_2}{t_1 + t_3}\right)\right\}$$

Comparing these shifts, it is clear that, if $t_1 > t_2 > t_3$, the shift of the demand curve of club 1 is smaller than the shift of club 2, which is again smaller than the shift of club 3, which confirms the general result in (6A.19).

Remarks

1. Expression (6A.18) also shows that, if the number of teams in the league is very high, the term between brackets approaches one, so the downward shift in demand for talent of all teams is more or less the same. It follows that in this case the invariance proposition still holds that revenue sharing does not affect the competitive balance. This result also confirms a well-known general proposition that a non-cooperative Nash equilibrium approaches the Walras equilibrium if the number of firms increases.

2. It is worth considering again the player market equilibrium in the fixed-supply Nash and Walras equilibria as presented by Figure 3.8, which is repeated here in Figure 6A.1. Assume that we are in the Nash equilibrium, at the point of intersection of the dotted non-linear demand curves, and the league introduces an equal, 50/50, sharing system. Not only will revenue sharing worsen the competitive balance, but the distribution of talent will be the same as for the market equilibrium in the Walras equilibrium model, with a salary level equal to zero. The reason is that, by a 50/50 sharing system, the negative externalities are fully neutralised as they are in a Walras model where the externalities are assumed to be internalised. No team is willing to pay for playing talent; it is the league that hires, allocates and pays the players. The

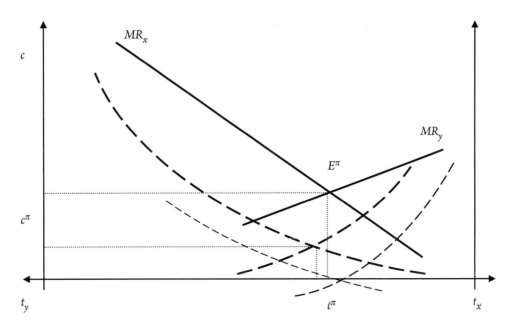

Figure 6A.1 Fixed-supply Walras and Nash equilibria

allocation of playing talents is optimal; total league revenue and profits are maximised (joint profit maximisation). As shown in Figure 6A.1, the 50/50 sharing arrangement causes a downward shift of both non-linear demand curves such that the new point of intersection is found at the horizontal axis, where the distribution of talent is the same as at the point of intersection of the linear demand curves, and where the unit cost of talent is zero.

3. Whereas the pool sharing system arrangement worsens the competitive balance if all clubs are profit maximisers, it is obvious that revenue sharing improves the competitive balance if clubs are **win maximisers**, even if the talent supply is flexible. As shown in Chapter 3, the flexible-supply Nash equilibrium and the fixed-supply Walras equilibrium are identical. Because the demand curves for talent are given by the net average revenue curves, the impact of pool sharing is the same as given by solution (6A.14). Because sharing increases the total revenue of those clubs that have a lower revenue than the average revenue in the league, and win-maximising clubs spend all their (net) revenue on talent, the result is an improved competitive balance.

4. It is also possible that, in one league, some clubs are profit maximisers and others are win maximisers. In the most likely case of the poorer

clubs being win maximisers, and the richer clubs being profit maximisers, the impact of revenue sharing is clear. Because the poor clubs will
increase their demand for talent and the rich clubs will reduce their
demand for talent, the impact of revenue sharing is a better competitive
balance.

Impact of revenue sharing on owner profits

If the impact of revenue sharing on the distribution of playing talents is different in the Nash equilibrium model compared with the Walras equilibrium
model, the impact of revenue sharing on profits can also be expected to be
different. This can be analysed starting again from equation (6A.14), where
the partial derivative of the after-sharing profit function with respect to μ is
given and which is repeated here:

$$
\frac{\partial \pi_i^*}{\partial \mu} = R_i[m, t_i^*] - \bar{R}[m, t^*] + \frac{\partial \bar{R}[m, t^*]}{\partial \mu} + \mu \left(\frac{\partial R_i[m, t_i^*]}{\partial \mu} - \frac{\partial \bar{R}[m, t^*]}{\partial \mu} \right)
$$

$$
- c^* \frac{\partial t_i^*}{\partial \mu} - t_i^* \frac{\partial c^*}{\partial \mu}. \tag{6A.20}
$$

Remember that a higher value of μ means less sharing and that a positive
sign of this equation means that more revenue sharing will lower club profits.
Whereas it is obvious that revenue sharing increases the profits of the small-
market clubs, the outcome for the large-market clubs is theoretically unde-
termined in both the flexible- and the fixed-supply models (see Késenne,
2007a).

In this section we will investigate only the impact of revenue sharing on the
profits of a medium-sized club with an average market size $\bar{m}$. For a medium-
sized club, the sum of the first five terms in equation (6A.20) is zero in
both the flexible-supply and the fixed-supply models. In the flexible-supply
model with an exogenous salary level, that is, $\frac{\partial c^*}{\partial \mu} = 0$, it has been shown
above that all clubs reduce their demand for talent, resulting in a more unbal-
anced competition, if revenues are shared. It follows that for a medium-sized
club $\frac{\partial t_i^*}{\partial \mu} > 0$. In the fixed-supply model, revenue sharing also worsens the
competitive balance but without changing the demand of a medium-sized
club. The equilibrium salary level will now decrease. This implies that for a
medium-sized club $\frac{\partial t_i^*}{\partial \mu} = 0$ and $\frac{\partial c^*}{\partial \mu} > 0$. It follows that it holds in both cases
that:

$$
\frac{\partial \pi_i^*}{\partial \mu} = -c^* \frac{\partial t_i^*}{\partial \mu} - t_i^* \frac{\partial c^*}{\partial \mu} < 0. \tag{6A.21}
$$

Revenue sharing only lowers the club's cost without changing its revenue, so the profits of a medium-sized club go up. Only if a decrease in total talent supply reduces the absolute quality of the league, or a worse competitive balance reduces public interest, might a negative effect on club revenue occur, but this is unlikely to offset the cost effect.

7

Salary caps

7.1 Introduction

After the abolition of the reservation system and the end of the monopsonistic exploitation of players in the North American major leagues in the
mid-1970s, player salaries went up dramatically, and, consequently, club
owner profits took a nosedive. In reaction to this profit squeeze, league
administrators and club owners looked for an alternative regulation system
to guarantee a reasonable profit rate. One of these alternatives is generally
known as salary caps. In Europe too, the introduction of salary caps was discussed, but primarily to keep clubs from running into heavy financial losses.
In fact, 'salary cap' is a misleading term. In most cases, a salary cap is not
a cap on the individual player's salary, but a cap on a club's season payroll,
which is the total amount that a club can spend on player salaries. But different types of salary caps can be distinguished. There are hard and soft
salary caps, or luxury taxes. The cap can be a fixed amount for every club in
the league, or it can be a percentage of a club's total budget; it can also be
at the same time a floor, so some cross-subsidisation is necessary to support
the low-budget clubs. Individual salary caps have also been imposed in
some leagues.

In this chapter, we will investigate how different types of salary caps affect
the distribution of talent, ticket prices, player salaries and owner profits in a
Walrasian fixed-supply model.

7.2 North American payroll cap

In a review article on cross-subsidisation in team sports, Fort and Quirk
(1995) conclude that a salary cap is the only cross-subsidisation scheme cur-
rently in use that can be expected to accomplish both the financial viability of
small-market teams and a better competitive balance in a league. The salary
cap these authors are dealing with is the typical payroll cap that is imposed
in North American major leagues, such as the NBA. It is a maximum amount
that clubs are allowed to spend on player salaries in one season. The cap is

calculated as a percentage (α) of average club revenue in the league during the previous season:

$$cap = \alpha\frac{\sum R_{i,-1}}{n} \qquad \alpha < 1. \tag{7.1}$$

It follows that the amount of the cap is the same for every club. The defined gross revenue of the league $\sum R_{i,-1}$ and, in particular, the percentage α are determined in collective bargaining agreements between the club owners and the players' associations. Lasting disagreements on the salary cap have ended in player strikes and owner lockouts in the North American major leagues. In fact, the NBA style of salary cap is not only a cap on the total payroll of a team, but also a floor. So, the low-budget clubs are forced to pay the fixed amount of the salary cap, with the implication that some cross-subsidisation among clubs can be required to accommodate the possible financial losses that this floor might cause to the low-budget clubs. In fact, this regulation system is a combination of a salary cap and a revenue-sharing arrangement. In theory, the clubs' equal spending on talent creates an equal distribution of talent and a lower salary level in the league (see Quirk and Fort, 1992). The problem with salary caps, though, is the enforcement of the salary cap, because there are many other ways to compensate players besides their regular salary.

In analysing the impact of this payroll cap, with and without the floor, we will again consider the profit-maximisation and the win-maximisation cases.

7.2.1 Salary caps and profit maximisation

In a competitive player labour market of a **profit-maximisation** league, imposing the payroll cap (7.1) means that:

$$ct_i \leq cap \quad \text{so} \quad c \leq \frac{cap}{t_i} \qquad \text{for all } i.$$

This implies that, graphically, the cap line is a simple hyperbolic function, which can be easily represented for a two-club model in Figure 7.1, where x is again the large-market club and y is the small-market club. We assume first that the salary cap is not effective for the small-market club, because it cannot afford to pay the amount of the cap.

If the payroll cap is not a floor, the cap does not affect the demand for talent of the low-budget club. As can be seen, the low-budget club's demand curve stays below the cap line. The high-budget club's demand curve is above the cap line; its payroll ct_x, which can be represented by a rectangle in Figure 7.1,

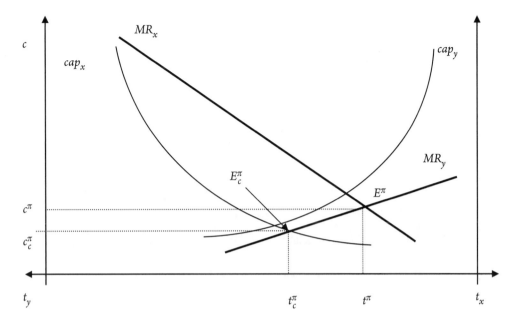

Figure 7.1 Payroll cap

has to stay below the hyperbolic function (cap_x). Obviously, the high-budget club will try to get as close as possible to its profit-maximising demand for talent. As a result, the hyperbole becomes its new demand curve for talent. The new market equilibrium is now found at E_c^π, the point of intersection of the marginal revenue curve of the low-budget club MR_y and the hyperbolic cap_x. The result is a more equal distribution of talent t_c^π and a lower salary level c_c^π.

Algebraically, it can be derived by equalising $MR_y = \frac{cap}{t_x}$:

$$m_y - m_y t_y = \frac{cap}{t_x} \quad and \quad m_y t_x = \frac{cap}{t_x} \qquad t_x = \sqrt{\frac{cap}{m_y}}.$$

The talents of club x are positively affected by the value of the cap and negatively affected by the market size of the opponent club y.

The impact of the salary cap on owner profits can be derived from Figure 7.2. A team's profits can be represented by the area below the demand curve and above the salary level. One can see that the move from equilibrium point E^π to E_c^π implies an increase in the profits of the low-budget club. The profits of the high-budget club also increase, because the gain in profits, caused by the lower salary level (the shaded rectangle in Figure 7.2), more than

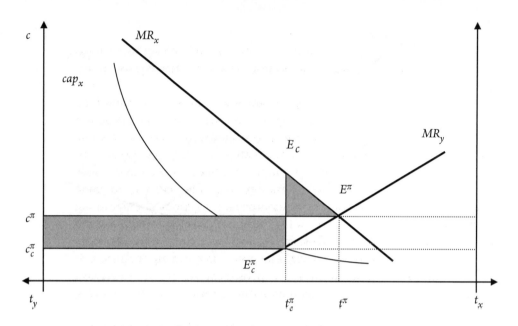

Figure 7.2 Payroll cap and owner profits

compensates for the loss in profits, caused by the lower talent demand (the shaded triangle in Figure 7.2).

If player salaries go down and owner profits go up, what happens to total league revenue? The loss in player salaries turns out to be larger than the gain in owner profits, because the new equilibrium deviates from the free market profit-maximising equilibrium. It follows that total league revenue comes down by imposing the salary cap, the loss being as large as the triangle $E_c E^\pi E_c^\pi$ in Figure 7.2. The reason is again a misallocation of playing talent. Owing to the salary cap, some talents are playing for the low-budget team when their marginal product would have been higher in the high-budget team (see Késenne, 2000b).

If the payroll cap is at the same time a floor, and some cross-subsidisation arrangements are in place, all clubs are forced to spend the same amount of money on playing talent. The equilibrium is then found where: $\frac{cap}{t_x} = \frac{cap}{t_y}$, with the result that $\frac{t_x}{t_y} = 1$, which is perfectly balanced competition. In Figure 7.1, the two hyperbolic functions are the new demand curves, and the new market equilibrium is reached at their point of intersection, which obviously results in a 50/50 distribution of talent and a lower salary level. The impact of this cap on the small-market team's profit is clearly positive, but it is theoretically unclear how the profit of the large-market team is affected, because the reduction in player salaries is smaller and the reduction of playing talent larger than without the floor (see Fort and Quirk, 1995). Total league revenue comes down again because of the inefficient allocation of talent.

Individual salary cap

So far, we have not mentioned the possibility of imposing an individual salary cap. It goes without saying that imposing an individual cap, below the market equilibrium level, will create excess demand on the player market. So, some talents can choose where to play, in the large- or in the small-market team. One can expect that most talents will prefer to play for the richer club, because this can provide more fringe benefits and greater exposure. As a consequence, an individual salary cap will worsen the competitive balance.

What if an individual salary cap is imposed together with a payroll cap (see Staudohar, 1999)? This is pictured in Figure 7.3, which can also be interpreted as a top-player model, as explained in section 3.3.3. The individual salary cap can be drawn as a horizontal line on the level of the individual cap ($capi$). It is obvious that, in order to be effective, this individual cap has to be lower than the salary level under the payroll cap at point E_c^π. Again the individual cap creates excess demand for playing talent. Given the new salary level $c = capi$, the new equilibrium point will be reached somewhere between the

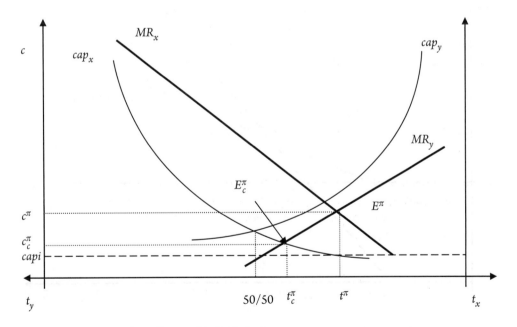

Figure 7.3 Payroll cap and individual salary cap

profit-maximising points of the large- and the small-market clubs, but it can be expected again that players will prefer to play for the large-market club and the better team. Comparing the outcomes of a payroll cap, with and without the individual cap, the profit-maximising large-market team will hire more talents when an individual cap is imposed. The small-market club is rationed and has to play with the talents that are left over. It follows that the individual cap creates a more unbalanced competition. Moreover, the profits of the large-market team will be higher, whereas it is unclear what happens to the profits of the small-market team. One positive outcome of an individual cap is that it can improve the salary distribution between star players and regular players, as can be derived from the segmented player market model in section 3.3.3.

Things get more complicated if one starts from the **two-decision variable model** introduced in Chapter 4, where club owners have to decide simultaneously on ticket price and talent demand. In Figure 7.4, where the two decision variables are found on the axes, the first-order conditions for profit maximisation $\pi_t = 0$ and $\pi_p = 0$ are drawn. With an exogenously given salary level, a payroll cap for the large-market team can be drawn as a horizontal line $t = cap/c$ below the profit-maximising equilibrium point E^π. By this horizontal

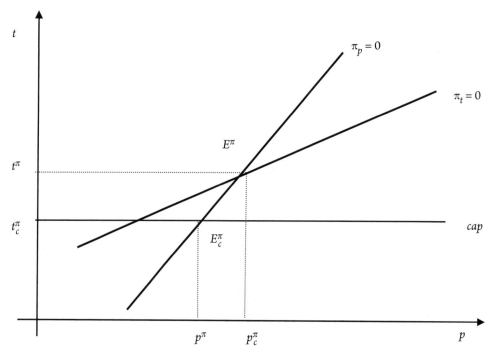

Figure 7.4 Payroll cap in a large-market team

cap line, the first-order condition $\pi_t = 0$ is no longer relevant. It follows that the optimal ticket price and talent demand are found in E_c^π at the point of intersection of the cap line at t_c^π and the locus $\pi_p = 0$, which indicates a lower ticket price and a lower demand for talent in the large-market team.

If the payroll cap is not a floor, it does not affect the small-market team directly. There will be only an indirect effect. Because the salary level is not exogenous in a competitive player market, a reduction in the market demand for talent will lower the market clearing salary level. This lower salary level will cause an upward shift of the locus $\pi_t = 0$.

As can be seen in Figure 7.5, the new equilibrium is reached at the point of intersection E_c^π of the locus $\pi_p = 0$ and the shifted locus $\pi_t = 0$. It follows that both ticket price and talent demand in the small-market team will go up.

If the payroll cap is at the same time a floor, the small-market club is forced to spend more money on salaries, with the extra money it receives from a cross-subsidisation arrangement. The cap line is now a horizontal line above the competitive market equilibrium in Figure 7.6, with the result that the small-market team will increase its ticket price from p^π to p_c^π.

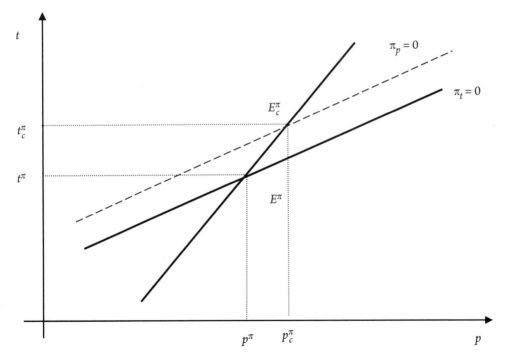

Figure 7.5 Payroll cap in a small-market team

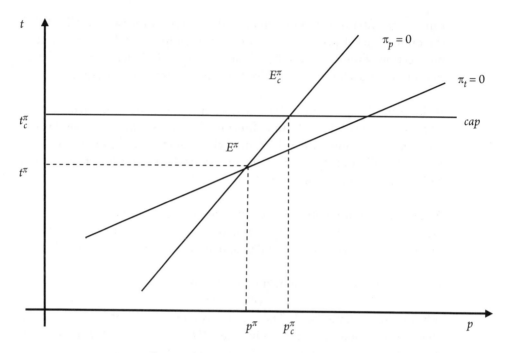

Figure 7.6 Payroll cap and floor in a small-market team

The conclusion is that a North American payroll cap, with or without a floor, improves the competitive balance and lowers the salary level in a profit-maximisation league. It has a different effect on the ticket price in the large- and the small-market teams.

Numerical example

Returning to the numerical example of a two-decision variable model in Chapter 4, and assuming that the large-market team's attendance function is:

$$A = \ln(1 + t) - p,$$

with profit function:

$$\pi = p\ln(1 + t) - p^2 - ct,$$

the first-order conditions for profit maximisation $\pi_p = 0$ and $\pi_t = 0$ are:

$$p = \frac{\ln(1 + t)}{2} \quad \text{and} \quad p = c(1 + t).$$

Table 7.1 Simulation results: North American salary cap

Large-market club	Free market equilibrium	Cap = 1.00 Same salary	Cap = 1.00 Lower salary
Salary level	0.10	0.10	0.09
Talents	12	10	11
Ticket price	1.30	1.10	1.08
Payroll	1.20	1.00	0.99
Attendance	1.26	1.29	1.40
Revenue	1.64	1.43	1.52
Profits	0.44	0.43	0.53

Starting from a given salary level equal to 0.10, the free market results are given for a number of variables in the first column of Table 7.1. One can see that the total payroll is 1.2. If we consider the case of a payroll cap of 1.0, which is not a floor and which is only relevant for this large-market team, and assuming further that the salary is exogenous and stays the same, the results are presented in the second column of Table 7.1. One can see now that, with the payroll staying below the cap, both the demand for talents and the ticket price decrease. In this example, attendance is up, because the positive effect of a lower ticket price is stronger than the negative effect of fewer talents. This result, however, is not generally true, because it depends on the relative size of the price elasticity and the talent elasticity of ticket demand. The same has to be said for total revenue and profits, which have gone down in this example.

The last column presents the results under the more interesting assumption that the market clearing salary level goes down from 0.10 to 0.09. The demand for talent and the ticket price are still lower, but attendance is up. Total revenue is down but profits are up compared with the free market outcome.

What is important here is that, in both cases, the demand for talent and the ticket price are lower under the payroll cap, and that there is no guarantee that a payroll cap will increase profits in a two-decision variable model.

7.2.2   Salary caps and win maximisation

If clubs are win maximisers, the impact of a payroll cap, with or without the floor, will be very similar to that in the profit-maximisation case as presented in Figure 7.1, where the marginal revenue curves are simply to be replaced by the net average revenue curves. However, the motivation of the league administrators in imposing the cap can be different. If clubs are win maximisers, the payroll cap is not primarily meant to guarantee a reasonable profit rate, but rather to force clubs to maintain a sound financial structure. Again, the cap will lower the salary level and improve the competitive balance. The large-market team will become profitable, even if it is not interested in making profits. In a win-maximisation league, the payroll cap can increase total league revenue, because it moves the allocation of talent closer to the profit-maximisation equilibrium, where talent is more efficiently allocated.

In the **two-decision variable model**, the impact of the payroll cap is presented in Figure 7.7 for a large-market team. Together with the first-order conditions, the zero-profit contour is also drawn. The team's initial equilibrium is given by point E^w, where talent is maximised given the zero-profit constraint. If a payroll cap is imposed, it can be represented again by a horizontal cap line $t = cap / c$ below the equilibrium talent level.

Now the large-market team has a choice: it can pocket the profits and set the profit-maximising ticket price p^{π}, or it can maximise attendance under

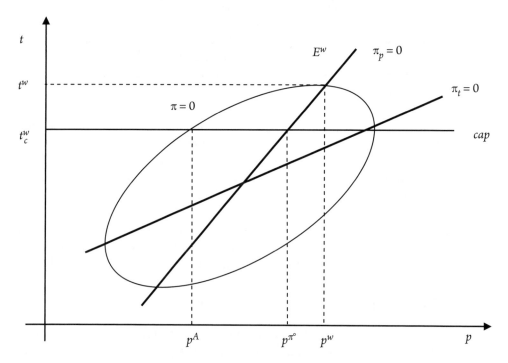

Figure 7.7 Payroll cap in a win-maximising large-market team

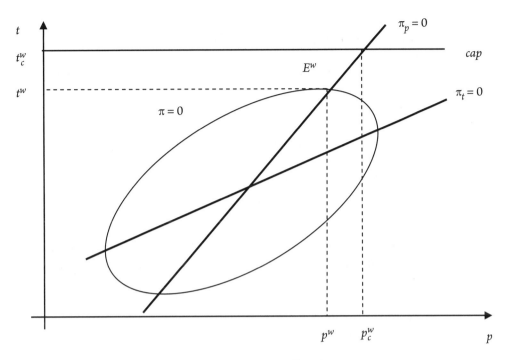

Figure 7.8 Payroll cap in a win-maximising small-market team

the zero-profit constraint by lowering the ticket price to p^A. Of course, it can also decide to go between these two extreme positions. In any case, the ticket price of the large-market team will be lower owing to the payroll cap.

If the payroll cap is also a floor, the small-market team, which receives a subsidy, will increase its ticket price, as can be seen in Figure 7.8. The subsidy allows the club to make a loss, so it can break outside the breakeven contour $\pi = 0$ and, maximising talent, set the ticket price at p_c^w.

If the payroll cap is not a floor, the cap is not effective and the small-market team is affected only indirectly. The cap causes a decrease of the equilibrium salary level, with the result that both the locus $\pi_t = 0$ and the breakeven contour $\pi = 0$ shift upward and a higher ticket price is set (see Késenne and Pauwels, 2006).

7.3 Soft cap and luxury tax

In section 7.2, it was assumed that the payroll cap was a hard cap, which means that a club's payroll is not, under any circumstance, allowed to exceed the value of the cap. However, in some North American major leagues, soft salary caps are imposed. Teams that pay more to their players than the value of the cap have to pay a tax, which is called a luxury tax.

Assume that a proportional tax is imposed on a club's payroll if the payroll exceeds the amount of the payroll cap. In this case, the profit function can be written as:

$$\pi_i = R[m_i, t_i] - (1 + \tau)ct_i \quad \text{if} \quad ct_i > cap.$$

The first-order condition for maximum profits is then:

$$\frac{\partial R_i}{\partial t_i} = c(1 + \tau).$$

If the tax is levied only on the high-budget team whose payroll exceeds the cap, then only the rich team will lower its demand for talent, with the result that the distribution of talent improves.

In the two-club model where x is again the high-budget team, the market equilibrium is given by:

$$\frac{1}{1 + \tau} \frac{\partial R_x}{\partial t_x} = c = \frac{\partial R_y}{\partial t_y}.$$

The competitive balance will improve compared with the pre-tax equilibrium. This can be illustrated in Figure 7.9, where the demand curve of the large-market club is kinked at the point where the payroll reaches the value of the cap.

If the market equilibrium point before the luxury tax is imposed is E^π, the after-tax equilibrium point is E_c^π. The competitive balance improves and the salary level comes down.

A variant of this luxury tax is a progressive tax on season club revenue as proposed by van der Burg and Prinz (2005), who show that it improves the distribution of talent. Although their proof starts from simplified revenue functions, it can easily be shown that this result holds in general for a season revenue function that is concave in the winning percentage. Starting from the profit function $\pi_i = R_i[m_i, t_i] - ct_i - c_i^0$, the first-order condition for maximum profits, if a progressive tax rate τ_i on total club revenue is imposed, can be written as:

$$(1 - \tau_i) \frac{\partial R_i}{\partial t_i} = c \quad \text{for all } i.$$

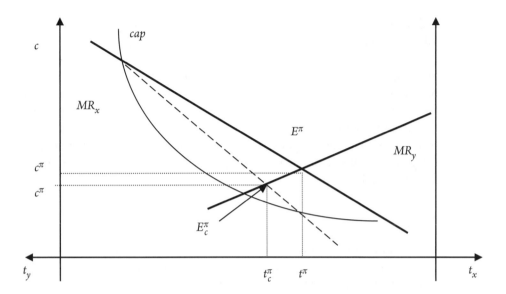

Figure 7.9 Luxury tax

Comparing this equation with the first-order condition before taxation, and given the concavity of the revenue functions, it is obvious that the large-budget team will lower its demand for talent more than the low-budget team if the progressive tax rate τ_i is higher for the large-budget club. It follows that the competitive balance in the league will improve. Obviously, given a constant supply of talent, the equilibrium salary level will come down.

Exactly the same results from imposing a luxury tax can be found under win maximisation.

7.4   G-14 payroll cap in European football

The G-14, which was the union of the 18 (originally 14) most successful football clubs in Europe (now it is called the European Club Association, ECA), proposed a payroll cap that deviates fundamentally from the North American cap in (7.1). The proposal, which was only a gentlemen's agreement, is to fix a maximum wage/turnover ratio or:

$$\frac{ct_i}{R_i} \leq \alpha \ \text{ so } \ cap_i = \alpha R_i \ \text{ with } \alpha < 1, \tag{7.2}$$

where α is a fixed wage/turnover ratio. Unlike the case for the North American cap, the maximum amount that a team can spend on player salaries is different for each team, so a different impact on competitive balance and salary level can also be expected.

Starting with **profit maximisation**, the G-14 salary cap shows some resemblance to the macroeconomic proposal of Weitzman (1984) to fight stagflation, which he called the 'share economy'. An implication of Weitzman's labour compensation system, which gives workers a percentage of a firm's revenue, is that the marginal revenue of labour is always higher than the marginal cost. Based on the payroll cap in (7.2), $MC_i = \alpha MR_i$ and the profit function can be written as:

$$\pi_i = (1 - \alpha)R_i - c_i^0,$$

so that all profit-maximising teams are willing to hire talent until the marginal revenue of playing talent is zero. If all playing talent is looking for the best-paying team, it can be shown that this type of salary cap worsens the competitive balance. If the G-14 payroll cap is binding for both the large- and the small-market teams, the new equilibrium distribution of talent is found at the point of intersection of the AR curves:

$$\frac{\alpha R_i}{t_i} = c \quad \text{or} \quad AR_i = c / \alpha \quad \text{for all } i. \tag{7.3}$$

It follows that the profit-maximisation equilibrium under a G-14 salary cap results in the same distribution of talent as in a win-maximisation league (in the absence of any capital compensation). As can be seen in Figure 7.10, this will cause a more unequal distribution of talent compared with the market equilibrium in a profit-maximisation league. However, the salary level that emerges after the introduction of the payroll cap is not found at the point of intersection of the AR curves, because the payroll is only a fixed percentage α of the average revenue. Given the main objective of the G-14 cap, the parameter α will be set low enough to be effective. In Figure 7.10, the new unit cost of talent, or salary level, is given by c_c^π.

Using the quadratic revenue functions $R_i = m_i t_i - 0.5 m_i t_i^2$ in a two-club model with $m_x > m_y$, the more unequal distribution of talent under a G-14 cap can be calculated, referring to the results found in Chapter 3, as:

$$\frac{t_x}{t_y} = \frac{2m_x - m_y}{2m_y - m_x} > \frac{m_x}{m_y}.$$

The player salary level can then be found as:

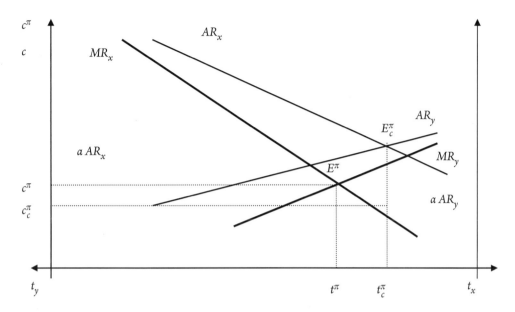

Figure 7.10 G-14 payroll cap in a profit-maximisation league (a)

$$c_c^\pi = \frac{\alpha R_i}{t_i} = \alpha(m_i - 0.5m_i t_i) = \alpha\frac{m_x m_y}{m_x + m_y}.$$

This result is based on the condition that the payroll cap is binding for both teams. It is possible, however, that the G-14 cap is not binding for the large-market team. It can be shown that the large-market team has a lower wage/turnover ratio than the small-market team:

$$\frac{c^\pi t_x^\pi}{R_x} < \frac{c^\pi t_y^\pi}{R_y}, \text{which can also be written as} \frac{c^\pi}{AR_x} < \frac{c^\pi}{AR_y}.$$

At the point of intersection of the MR curves, the AR of the large-market team is higher than the AR of the small-market team.

If the payroll cap is not relevant for the large-market team but only affects the payroll of the small-market team, the result will also be a more unbalanced distribution of playing talent, as can be seen in Figure 7.11.

The large-market team's demand curve for talent is still given by the marginal revenue curve MR_x, while the small-market club's demand is given by the curve αAR_y. The new market equilibrium is found at the point of intersection E_c^π, with a more unequal distribution of talent also. One can conclude that a G-14 payroll cap worsens the competitive balance in a profit-maximisation league.

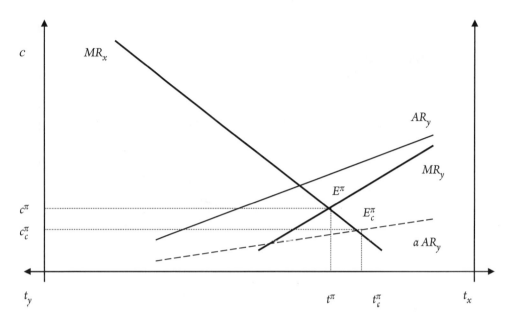

Figure 7.11 G-14 payroll cap in a profit-maximisation league (b)

Because the G-14 salary cap is only a gentlemen's agreement, Dietl et al. (2006) have investigated under what conditions such a voluntary salary cap agreement is self-enforcing. Based on their theoretical model, the teams' valuation of future profits and the importance of competitive balance for public interest add to the self-enforcing character.

In a **win-maximisation** league, where a club's demand for talent is given by the net average revenue curve (NAR), the free market equilibrium is found where:

$$NAR_i = \frac{R_i - c_i^0}{t_i} = c \quad \text{for all } i.$$

If the G-14 cap is imposed, and if the cap is relevant for both teams, the market equilibrium is again given by (7.3). Comparing the equilibria before and after, different outcomes are possible, depending on the size of the fixed capital cost.

If the capital cost of each team is assumed to be proportional to team revenue with the same proportionality factor k:

$$c_i^0 = kR_i \quad \text{so} \quad NAR_i = (1 - k)AR_y$$

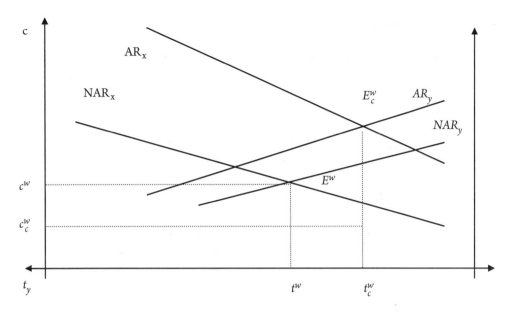

Figure 7.12 G-14 payroll cap in a win-maximisation league

the distribution of talent will be the same as before. However, if k is higher, or the wage/turnover ratio $(1-k)$ is lower, in the large-market team, the G-14 cap worsens the competitive balance in a win-maximisation league. This can be seen by considering the shifts of the demand curves of the large- and small-market teams in Figure 7.12. If the competitive market equilibrium is given by E^w at the point of intersection of net average revenue curves, the equilibrium after the introduction of the payroll cap is point E^w_c.

It follows that the G-14 salary cap will also worsen the competitive balance in a win-maximisation league. Given that the major concern of the G-14 is the sound financial structure of European football clubs, the point of reference for analysing the impact of a payroll cap is not the breakeven point of all clubs. If the financial losses of the small-market clubs are, on average, larger than those of the large-market clubs, it is obvious that in this case also the G-14 payroll cap worsens the competitive balance (see Késenne, 2003).

For an analysis of the effects of salary caps in professional team sports on social welfare, see Dietl, Lang and Rathke (2009).

7.5 Conclusion

All problems of enforcing salary caps aside, one can conclude that the North American style of payroll cap, which imposes the same maximum amount on all clubs, has a favourable effect on competitive balance. It also lowers the labour cost of clubs, which helps professional teams located in weak-drawing markets to maintain financial viability. In general, a salary cap will not bring ticket prices down. Small-market clubs, whether they are profit or win maximisers, can be expected to increase their ticket prices. If the cap is also a floor, it is not guaranteed that a salary cap will increase the large-market clubs' profits.

The G-14 type of payroll cap which fixes a maximum wage/turnover ratio, and thus a different amount of cap for each team, can be expected to worsen the competitive balance. But it does reach its major objective, which is to restore the troubled financial structure of many clubs.

EXERCISES 7

7.1 Starting from the revenue functions $R_x = 160t_x - 100t_x^2$ and $R_x = 120t_y - 100t_y^2$, with $t_x + t_y = 1$, the profit-maximisation equilibrium is $\frac{t_x}{t_y} = \frac{0.6}{0.4} = 1.5$ and $c^\pi = 40$. The payroll of the large-market club is then 24 and of the small-market club 16. Assuming that a payroll cap of 20 is imposed by the league, what will be the distribution of talent and the salary level?

7.2 Starting from the same profit-maximisation model as in exercise 7.1, and assuming that a soft salary cap is fixed at 20, and that the large-market club, exceeding the value of the cap, has to pay a luxury tax rate of $\tau = 0.1$, what will be the distribution of talent and the salary level?

7.3 Starting again from the same profit-maximisation model as in exercise 7.1:

- Calculate the wage/turnover ratio of both clubs.
- If the league is imposing a maximum value of the wage/turnover ratio of 30 per cent, what will be the new market equilibrium distribution of talent and the salary level?

7.4 Starting again from the same profit-maximisation model as in exercise 7.1, and assuming that the maximum wage/turnover ratio is fixed at 45 per cent, so that it is not binding for the large-market club, derive the equilibrium distribution of talent and the salary level.

7.5 With the same revenue functions as in exercise 7.1, but now with win-maximising clubs, assume that for the capital cost of both clubs it holds that $c_i^0 = 0.20R_i$. If a maximum wage/turnover ratio of 60 per cent is imposed, what will be the equilibrium distribution of talent and the salary level?

Answers to exercises

Exercises 1

1.1 A profit-maximising club will hire talent until marginal revenue equals marginal cost. $\partial R/\partial t = 10 - 2t = \partial C/\partial t = 2$, so $t_1 = 4$. Profits are $\pi_1 = R_1 - C_1 = 24 - 8 = 16$.

1.2 A revenue-maximising club will hire talents until marginal revenue is zero. $\partial R/\partial t = 10 - 2t = 0$, so $t_2 = 5$. The club is still profitable: $\pi_2 = R_2 - C_2 = 25 - 10 = 15$.

1.3 A win-maximising club, under the breakeven condition, will hire talent until total revenue equals total cost. $R = 10t - t^2 = C = 2t$, so the quadratic equation $8t - t^2 = 0$ has to be solved. This equation has two solutions, $t_4 = 8$ and $t_4' = 0$. A win-maximising club will obviously choose the first solution. One can check that profits are indeed zero: $\pi_3 = R_3 - C_3 = 16 - 16 = 0$.

1.4 If a linear combination of profits and wins $\pi + at$ is maximised with $a = 3$, the first-order condition is $11 - 2t = 0$, so $t_4 = 5.5$ and $\pi_4 = R_4 - C_4 = 24.75 - 11 = 13.75$.

Exercises 2

2.1 If the club owner's objective is to make as much profit as possible, the optimality condition is given by $\frac{\partial R}{\partial p} = \frac{\partial C}{\partial p} = 0$. If total revenue is $R = pA = 5p - 0.5p^2$, the optimality condition is $\frac{\partial R}{\partial p} = 5 - p = 0$, so the optimal ticket price is 5 euros and attendance is 25 000. Total revenue is 125 000 euros. However, if the stadium can receive only 20 000 spectators, the manager will set the price at 6 euros by solving $2 = 5 - 0.5p$. Total revenue is 120 000 euros.

2.2 The optimality condition under profit maximisation with $R = (p + 4)A = 20 + 3p - 0.5p^2$ is now $\frac{\partial R}{\partial p} = 3 - p = 0$, so that the optimal ticket price is 3 euros and attendance is 35 000. Total revenue is then $7 \times 35\,000 = 245\,000$ euros. If the stadium can hold only 20 000 fans,

Table A.1 Answer to exercise 2.4

p	A	R	C = 2		C = 3		C = 4	
			C	π	C	π	C	π
3	3.5	10.5	8	2.5	12	−1.5	16	−5.5
4	3	12	8	4	12	0	16	−4
5	2.5	12.5	8	4.5	12	0.5	16	−3.5
6	2	12	8	4	12	0	16	−4
7	1.5	10.5	8	2.5	12	−1.5	16	−5.5

the manager will again set the price at 6 euros, so total revenue is now $10 \times 20\,000 = 200\,000$ euros.

2.3 Given the ticket demand function $p = 10 - 2A$, and a maximum ticket price of 2 euros, the number of spectators can be found by solving $2 = 10 - 2A$, so $A = 40\,000$ and team revenue is $80\,000$ euros.

2.4 Table A.1 presents the club's profits for every ticket price and every unit cost of talent.

One observes that, whatever the cost of talent, the ticket price that maximises profit is always the same, $p = 5$. What this simple numerical example shows is that the unit cost of talent or the players' salary level does not affect the profit-maximising ticket price. Note that profit maximisation also means loss minimisation in the case where there is no ticket price that makes the club profitable.

2.5 Because total revenue is given by $R = 12q_r - 2q_r^2$, the marginal revenue is $\frac{\partial R}{\partial q_r} = 12 - 4q_r$. With a marginal cost that is zero, the optimality condition is given by: $12 - 4q_r = 0$, so that $q_{r1} = 3$ and $p_{r1} = 6$. Total revenue $R_1 = 18$ and profit $\pi_1 = 15$.

2.6 In a competitive market of TV rights, the equilibrium is found where demand equals supply. The supply curve, being the marginal cost curve, is $p_r = 0.4q_r$. It follows that the optimum is found where $12 - 2q_r = 0.4q_r$, so that $q_{r2} = 5$ and $p_{r2} = 2$. Total revenue $R_2 = 10$, total cost $C_2 = 7$ and profit $\pi_2 = 3$. Comparing these results with the previous ones, league profits are much lower, so that the league and the clubs are better off under pooling, but the price is much lower and the output higher, so the spectators are better off under decentralised selling in a competitive market.

2.7 The total revenue of the broadcast company can be found to be $R = pq + R_a = 14q_s - 0.5q_s^2$, so the first-order condition is: $MR = 14 - qs = MC = 0$ and $q_{s1} = 14$ and $p_{s1} = 3$. The revenue from advertising is 56; the revenue from viewing is 42. Total revenue is 98, so the total profit is 48. In the case of free-to-air broadcasting, the price is zero and the number of spectators will be 20. Although revenue from advertising is now 80, which is higher than under pay-per-view, it is also the only revenue source, so total profit is 30. We can derive that the company will choose pay-per-view. Obviously, the spectator would prefer the free-to-air broadcasting of games.

Exercises 3

3.1 Under profit maximisation, the player market equilibrium can be found from: $12 - 12t_x = 8 - 8(1 - t_x)$, which results in: $t_x^\pi = 0.6$ and $t_y^\pi = 0.4$ or $\frac{w_x^\pi}{w_y^\pi} = 1.5$. The market clearing unit cost of talent, which is equal to the marginal revenue in both clubs, can be calculated as $c_\pi = 12 - 12(0.6) = 4.8$. The total revenue of club x is then equal to: $R_x^\pi = 12(0.6) - 6(0.6)^2 = 7.2 - 2.16 = 5.04$. The total revenue of club y is: $R_y^\pi = 8(0.4) - 4(0.4)^2 = 3.2 - 0.64 = 2.56$, so the total league revenue is: $R^\pi = 5.04 + 2.56 = 7.6$. The profits of club x are: $\pi_x = 5.04 - 0.6(4.8) = 2.16$. The profits of club y are: $\pi_Y = 2.56 - 0.4(4.8) = 0.64$.

3.2 Under win maximisation the player market equilibrium can be found from: $12 - 6t_x = 8 - 4(1 - t_x)$, which results in: $t_x^w = 0.8$ and $t_y^w = 0.2$ or $\frac{w_x^w}{w_y^w} = 4$. The competitive balance is more unequal than in a profit-maximisation league. The market clearing unit cost of talent, which is equal to the average revenue in both clubs, can be calculated as: $c_w = 12 - 6(0.8) = 7.2$, which is higher than under profit maximisation. The total revenue of club x is then equal to: $R_x^w = 12(0.8) - 6(0.8)^2 = 5.76$. The total revenue of club y is: $R_y^w = 8(0.2) - 4(0.2)^2 = 1.44$, so the total league revenue is: $R^w = 5.76 + 1.44 = 7.20$, which shows that win maximisation causes a loss of total league revenue compared with profit maximisation.

3.3 Based on the equation, derived in the Appendix to Chapter 3, $t_i^w = 2t_i^\pi - 0.5$, the winning percentages can be calculated as shown in Table A.2.

Table A.2 Answer to exercise 3.3

w_i^π	$w_i^w = 2w_i^\pi - 1/5$
0.70	0.90
0.60	0.70
0.55	0.60
0.50	0.50
0.35	0.20
0.30	0.10
3.00	3.00

It is clear that the standard deviation of the win percentages in the win-maximisation league is larger than the standard deviation in the profit-maximisation league.

3.4 Under these conditions the result can be found from $MR_x = AR_y$: $12 - 12t_x = 8 - 4(1 - t_x)$, so: $t_x^{\pi w} = 0.5$ and $t_y^{\pi w} = 0.5$ and $c_{\pi w} = 6$.

3.5 If the small-market club is more win orientated than the large-market club, the result can be found from: $12 - 12t_x = 8 - 8(1 - t_x) + 4$, so: $t_x = 0.4$ and $t_y = 0.6$ and $c = 7.2$.

3.6 The reaction functions in the Nash equilibrium model are: $(12 - 12w_x) \frac{t_y}{(t_x + t_y)^2} = c = (8 - 8w_y) \frac{t_x}{(t_x + t_y)^2}$. Given that the supply of talent is constant and can be normalised to equal unity, this equation simplifies to: $(12w_y)t_y = c = (8w_x)t_x$ and $12t_y^2 = 8t_x^2$, so the competitive balance is: $\frac{w_x^\pi}{w_y^\pi} = \sqrt{\frac{12}{8}} = \sqrt{1.5} = 1.22$. The equilibrium salary level can then be derived from: $t_x + t_y = 1$ or $\sqrt{c/12} + \sqrt{c/8} = 1$, so $c = \frac{12 \times 8}{(\sqrt{12} + \sqrt{8})^2} = 96/6.29^2 = 2.43$.

Exercises 4

4.1 The unconstrained profit-maximising equilibrium is found at the point of intersection of the two first-order conditions: $\frac{\partial \pi}{\partial t} = \frac{p}{4\sqrt{t}} - 1 = 0$ $\frac{\partial \pi}{\partial p} = \frac{\sqrt{t}}{2} - 1 = 0$, which results in: $t^* = 4$ and $p^* = 8$. The ticket price is above the maximum ticket price, so the new equilibrium is found at the point of intersection of the locus $\pi_t = 0$ and the ticket price constraint: $\frac{6}{2\sqrt{t}} = 1$, so $t^{**} = 2.25$.

4.2 In this case, the optimal ticket price and the hiring of talent can be found at the point of intersection of the price line and the stadium capacity constraint.

The stadium capacity constraint can be written as: $t = \frac{p^2}{4}$ or $p = 2\sqrt{t}$, so the optimum is found where: $2\sqrt{t} = 8$, so $t^* = 16$.

Exercises 5

5.1 The equilibrium of a non-discriminating profit-maximising monopsonist is found by the solution of: $MR = 2.8 - 2t = MC = 0.4 + t$, so $t_m^\pi = 0.8$. Using the supply function, the salary level can be found as $c_m^\pi = 0.8$. The marginal revenue $MR_m^\pi = 1.2$, so the rate of monopsonistic exploitation (RMC) can be calculated as $RME = 1 - \frac{c_m^\pi}{MR_m^\pi} = 0.33$.

5.2 The equilibrium of a discriminating profit-maximising monopsonist is found by: $MR = 2.8 - 2t = MC = 0.4 + 0.5t$, so $t_{dm}^\pi = 0.96$. All playing talents are paid a different salary level.

5.3 The equilibrium demand for talent of a win-maximising non discriminating monopsonist is found by solving: $AR = 2.8 - t = S = 0.4 + 0.5t$, so $t_m^w = 1.6$. If the monopsonist does not discriminate, he is paying every talent: $c_m^w = 1.2$. This is above marginal revenue, which can even be negative: $MR_m^w = -0.4$.

Exercises 6

6.1 The revenue functions after sharing can be written as: $R_x^* = 0.8R_x + 0.2R_y$ and $R_y^* = 0.8R_y + 0.2R_x$. The corresponding marginal revenues are then, knowing that $t_x + t_y = 1$: $MR_x^* = 0.8(12 - 12t_x) - 0.2(8 - 8t_y) = 9.6 - 11.2t_x$ and $MR_y^* = 0.8(8 - 8t_y) - 0.2(12 - 12t_x) = 6.4 - 8.8t_y$. The market equilibrium, or the point of intersection of the two demand curves for talent after sharing, is found by the solution of: $9.6 - 11.2t_x = 6.4 - 8.8t_y$, which results in $t_x = 3/5$ and $t_y^* = 2/5$, which is the same as the distribution of talent before sharing. The salary level is $c^* = 9.6 - 11.2(0.6) = 9.6 - 6.7 = 2.9$, which is lower than the salary level before sharing.

6.2 Table A.3 presents the main results for the three values of the share parameter; if $\mu = 1$, there is no sharing; if $\mu = 0$, there is equal sharing.

One can see that revenue sharing increases the poor club's profit. It decreases the rich club's profit, because the rich club's profit is larger than the average budget in the league. Total league profits go up, owing to the sharing arrangement. It can also be seen that the distribution of talent before sharing ($\mu = 1$) is the same as after sharing according to the invariance proposition.

Table A.3 Answer to exercise 6.2

μ	t_x/t_y	R_x	R_y	$\bar{R}$	c	C_x	C_y	π_x	π_y	π
1	8/2	96	12	54	40	32	8	64	4	68
0.5	8/2	75	33	54	20	16	4	59	29	88
0	8/2	54	54	54	0	0	0	54	54	108

Remember that a pool share parameter of $\mu = 0.5$ means that the large club keeps 75 per cent of its revenue and receives 25 per cent of the small clubs' revenue. If $\mu = 0$, which means equal sharing, all clubs' revenues and profits are equal, and the market clearing unit cost of talent is zero; clubs are no longer willing to pay for talent.

6.3 After sharing, the average revenue functions are: $AR_x^* = 160 - 100t_x - \frac{1}{2}(160 - 140) = 150 - 100t_x$ and $AR_y^* = 120 - 100t_y - \frac{1}{2}(120 - 140) = 130 - 100t_y$, so that under win maximisation a more equal distribution of talent is reached, $t_x^*/t_y^* = 0.6/0.4$.

Exercises 7

7.1 Because the salary cap is relevant only for the large-market club, the new equilibrium is found as the solution of: $\frac{20}{t_x} = 120 - 200t_y$, so the following quadratic function has to be solved: $200t_x^2 - 80t_x - 20 = 0$. The solution is $t_x^c = \frac{80 + \sqrt{6400 + 4(4000)}}{400} = 0.57$, so $\frac{t_x^c}{t_y^c} = \frac{0.57}{0.43} = 1.32$, which is a more equal competitive balance. The new salary level is $c^c = \frac{20}{0.57} = 35$, which is lower.

7.2 The new equilibrium can be found by the solution of: $(1 - 0.1)(160 - 200t_x) = 120 - 200t_y$, so $t_x^c = 0.59$, so $\frac{t_x^c}{t_y^c} = \frac{0.59}{0.41} = 1.44$. The salary level is then $c^c = 38$.

7.3 The wage/turnover ratio can be calculated for the large- and the small-market clubs as $\frac{c_x t_x^c}{R_x^c} = 0.4$ and $\frac{c_y t_y^c}{R_y^c} = 0.5$. If the maximum wage/turnover ratio is 0.3, the new market equilibrium can be found as the solution of $0.3AR_x = 0.3AR_y$ or $160 - 100t_x = 120 - 100(1 - t_x)$, so $\frac{t_x^c}{t_y^c} = \frac{0.7}{0.3} = 2.3$ and $c^c = 0.3(160 - 70) = 27$. One can verify that, in this equilibrium, the wage/turnover ratios of both clubs are equal to 0.3.

7.4 In this case the demand for talent of the profit-maximising large-market club is given by the marginal revenue. The new market equilibrium is then found as the solution of: $MR_x = 0.45AR_y$ or $160 - 200t_x = 0.45(120 - 100(1 - t_x))$, so $\frac{t_x^c}{t_y^c} = \frac{0.62}{0.38} = 1.63$ and $c^c = 160 - 200(0.62) = 36$. In this case, the wage/turnover ratio of the small-market club is 0.44. The wage/turnover ratio of the large-market club is 0.36.

7.5 In a free market, the distribution of talent is found by solving $NAR_x = NAR_y$: $(1 - 0.20)AR_x = (1 - 0.20)AR_y$, so $\frac{t_x^c}{t_y^c} = \frac{0.7}{0.3} = 2.3$. This talent distribution is not affected by imposing a G-14 cap, because the capital cost is proportional to club revenue and the proportionality factor is the same in each club. The solution with the cap is given by $AR_x = AR_y$, which is obviously the same as without the cap. The free market salary level is $c^w = (1 - 0.20)AR^w = (1 - 0.20)90 = 72$. With this salary level, the wage/turnover ratios, which are the same in both clubs for obvious reasons, are equal to: $\frac{c^w t_x^c}{R_x^w} = \frac{50.4}{63} = \frac{c^w t_y^c}{R_y^w} = \frac{21.6}{27} = 0.8$. Because this is too high, the salary level has been brought down to: $c^c = 0.60AR^w = 0.60(90) = 54$.

References and selected bibliography

Akerlof, G. and J. Yellen (1986), *Efficiency Wage Models of the Labor Market*, Cambridge: Cambridge University Press.

Alexander, D. (2001), 'Major League Baseball: Monopoly Pricing and Profit Maximizing Behavior', *Journal of Sports Economics*, 2 (4), 356–68.

Andreff, W. (1989), *Economie Politique du Sport*, Paris: Editions Dalloz.

Andreff, W. (2011), *Recent Developments in the Economics of Sport*, Vols I and II, Cheltenham, UK and Northampton, MA, USA: Edward Elgar Publishing.

Andreff, W. and J.-F. Bourg (2006), 'Broadcasting Rights and Competition in European Football', in C. Jeanrenaud and S. Késenne (eds), *Sports and the Media*, Cheltenham, UK and Northampton, MA, USA: Edward Elgar Publishing, pp. 37–70.

Andreff, W. and S. Szymanski (2006), *Handbook of Sports Economics*, Cheltenham, UK and Northampton, MA, USA: Edward Elgar Publishing.

Atkinson, S., L. Stanley and J. Tschirhart (1988), 'Revenue Sharing as an Incentive in an Agency Problem: An Example from the National Football League', *RAND Journal of Economics*, 19 (1), 27–43.

Baade, R. (1996), 'Professional Sports as Catalysts for Metropolitan Economic Development', *Journal of Urban Affairs*, 18 (1), 1–17.

Barros, C., M. Ibrahimo and S. Szymanski (eds) (2002), *Transatlantic Sports: The Comparative Economics of North American and European Sports*, Cheltenham, UK and Northampton, MA, USA: Edward Elgar Publishing.

Borghans, L. and L. Groot (2005), 'The Competitive Balance Based on Team Quality', Working paper, Utrecht School of Economics, University of Utrecht.

Borland, J. and R. Macdonald (2003), 'Demand for Sport', *Oxford Review of Economic Policy*, 19 (4), 478–503.

Bourg, J.-F. and J.-J. Gouguet (1998), *Analyse Economique du Sport*, Paris: Presses Universitaires de France.

Buchanan, J. (1965), 'An Economic Theory of Clubs', *Economica*, 32 (125), 1–14.

Buraimo, B. and R. Simmons (2009), 'A Tale of Two Audiences: Spectators, Television Viewers and Outcome Uncertainty in Spanish Football', *Journal of Economics and Business*, 61, 326–38.

Burg, T. van der (1996), 'Het Voetbalmonopolie', *Economisch-Statistische Berichten*, 81 (4070), 710–11.

Burg, T. van der and A. Prinz (2005), 'Progressive Taxation as a Measure for Improving Competitive Balance', *Scottish Journal of Political Economy*, 52 (1), 65–74.

Cairns, J., N. Jennett and P. Sloane (1986), 'The Economics of Professional Team Sports: A Survey of Theory and Evidence', *Journal of Economic Studies*, 13 (1), 3–80.

Coase, R. (1960), 'The Problem of Social Cost', *Journal of Law and Economics*, 3, 1–44.

Coates, D., B. Humphreys and L. Zhou (2012), 'Outcome Uncertainty, Reference-Dependent Preferences and Live Game Attendance', Department of Economics paper, UMBC, Baltimore, MD.

Commission of the European Communities (2007), *White Paper on Sports*, COM(2007) 391 final, Brussels: Commission of the European Communities.

Dabscheck, B. (1975), 'Sporting Equality: Labour Market versus Product Market Control', *Journal of Industrial Relations*, 17 (2), 174–90.

Demmert, H. (1973), *The Economics of Professional Team Sports*, Lexington, MA: Lexington Books, D.C. Heath.

Dietl, H. and T. Hasan (2007), 'Pay-TV versus Free-TV: A Model of Sports Broadcasting Rights Sales', *Eastern Economic Journal*, 33 (3), 405–20.

Dietl, H. and M. Lang (2008), 'The Effect of Gate Revenue Sharing on Social Welfare', *Contemporary Economic Policy*, 26 (3), 448–59.

Dietl, H., E. Franck and S. Nüesch (2006), 'Are Voluntary Salary Cap Agreements Self-Enforcing?', *European Sport Management Quarterly*, 6 (1), 23–34.

Dietl, H., E. Franck and M. Lang (2008), 'Overinvestment in Team Sports Leagues: A Contest Theory Model', *Scottish Journal of Political Economy*, 55 (3), 353–68.

Dietl, H., M. Lang and A. Rathke (2009), 'The Effects of Salary Caps in Professional Team Sports on Social Welfare', *BE Journal of Economic Analysis and Policy*, 9 (7).

Dietl, H., M. Lang and S. Werner (2009), 'Social Welfare in Sports Leagues with Profit-Maximizing and/or Win-Maximizing Clubs', *Southern Economic Journal*, 76 (2), 375–96.

Dietl, H., M. Grossmann and M. Lang (2011), 'Competitive Balance and Revenue Sharing in Sports Leagues with Win-Maximizing Teams', *Journal of Sports Economics*, 12 (3), 284–308.

Dobson, S. and J. Goddard (2001), *The Economics of Football*, Cambridge: Cambridge University Press.

Downward, P. and A. Dawson (2000), *The Economics of Professional Team Sports*, London and New York: Routledge.

El-Hodiri, M. and J. Quirk (1971), 'An Economic Model of a Professional Sports League', *Journal of Political Economy*, 79, 1302–19.

European Court of Justice (1995), *Union royale belge des sociétés de football association ASBL v Jean-Marc Bosman, Royal club liégeois SA v Jean-Marc Bosman and others and Union des associations européennes de football (UEFA) v Jean-Marc Bosman*, Case C-415/93, European Court reports 1995 Page I-04921, http://eur-lex.europa.eu/LexUriServ/LexUriServ.do?uri=CELEX:61993J0415:EN:HTML (accessed 22 December 2006).

Falconieri, S., F. Palomino and J. Sákovics (2004), 'Collective versus Individual Sale of Television Rights in League Sports', *Journal of the European Economic Association*, 2 (5), 833–62.

Feess, E. and G. Muehlheusser (2003a), 'Transfer Fee Regulations in European Football', *European Economic Review*, 47, 645–68.

Feess, E. and G. Muehlheusser (2003b), 'The Impact of Transfer Fees on Professional Sports: An Analysis of the New Transfer System for European Football', *Scandinavian Journal of Economics*, 105 (1), 139–54.

Feess, E. and F. Stähler (2009), 'Revenue Sharing in Professional Sports Leagues', *Scottish Journal of Political Economy*, 56 (2), 255–65.

Ferguson, D., K. Stewart, J. Jones and A. Le Dressay (1991), 'The Pricing of Sport Events: Do Teams Maximize Profits?', *Journal of Industrial Economics*, 39 (3), 297–310.

FIFA–EU Transfer Agreement (2001), European Commission, Brussels.

Fizel, J. (ed.) (2006), *Handbook of Sports Economics Research*, London: M.E. Sharpe.

Fizel, J., L. Gustafson and J. Hadley (eds) (1996), *Baseball Economics: Current Research*, Westport, CT: Greenwood Press.

Fizel, J., L. Gustafson and J. Hadley (eds) (1999), *Sports Economics: Current Research*, London: Praeger.

Forrest, D. and R. Simmons (2002), 'Outcome Uncertainty and Attendance Demand in Sport: The Case of English Soccer', *The Statistician*, 51 (2), 229–41.

Forrest, D. and R. Simmons (2006), 'New Issues in Attendance Demand: The Case of the English Football League', *Journal of Sports Economics*, 7 (3), 247–66.

Fort, R. (2011), *Sports Economics*, 3rd edn, Englewood Cliffs, NJ: Prentice Hall.

Fort, R. and J. Fizel (eds) (2004), *International Sports Economics Comparisons*, Westport, CT: Praeger.

Fort, R. and J. Quirk (1995), 'Cross-Subsidization, Incentives and Outcomes in Professional Team Sports Leagues', *Journal of Economic Literature*, 33 (3), 1265–99.

Fort, R. and J. Quirk (2004), 'Owner Objectives and Competitive Balance', *Journal of Sports Economics*, 5 (1), 20–32.

Frick, B. (2003), 'Contest Theory and Sport', *Oxford Review of Economic Policy*, 19 (4), 512–29.

Garcia, J. and P. Rodriguez (2002), 'The Determinants of Football Match Attendance Revisited: Empirical Evidence from the Spanish Football League', *Journal of Sports Economics*, 3 (1), 18–38.

Garcia-del-Barrio, P. and S. Szymanski (2009), 'Goal! Profit Maximization versus Win Maximization in Soccer', *Review of Industrial Organization*, 34, 45–68.

Gerrard, B. (ed.) (2006), *The Economics of Association Football*, Cheltenham, UK and Northampton, MA, USA: Edward Elgar Publishing.

Goossens, K. (2006), 'National Measure of Seasonal Imbalance for Team Sports', Discussion paper, Economics Department, University of Antwerp.

Goossens, K. and S. Késenne (2007), 'National Dominance in European Football Leagues', in M. Parent and T. Slack (eds), *International Perspectives on the Management of Sport*, Burlington, MA: Elsevier, pp. 127–48.

Gratton, C. and P. Taylor (2000), *Economics of Sport and Recreation*, London: Spon Press.

Haan, M., R. Koning and A. van Witteloostuijn (2005), 'Institutional Change in European Soccer: A Theoretical Analysis of the Effects on Competitive Balance and the Quality of National Competitions', Discussion paper, Department of Economics, University of Groningen.

Hendricks, W. (ed.) (1997), *Advances in the Economics of Sport*, Vol. 2, Greenwich, CT: JAI Press.

Hoehn, T. and D. Lancefield (2003), 'Broadcasting in Sport', *Oxford Review of Economic Policy*, 19 (4), 552–68.

Hoehn, T. and S. Szymanski (1999), 'The Americanisation of European Football', *Economic Policy*, 28 (April), 207–40.

Humphreys, B. (2002), 'Alternative Measures of Competitive Balance', *Journal of Sports Economics*, 3 (2), 133–48.

Janssens, P. and S. Késenne (1986), 'Belgian Soccer Attendances', *Tijdschrift voor Economie en Management*, 32, 305–15.

Jeanrenaud, C. and S. Késenne (eds) (1999), *Competition Policy in Professional Sports*, Antwerp: Standaard Editions.

Jeanrenaud, C. and S. Késenne (eds) (2006), *Sports and the Media*, Cheltenham, UK and Northampton, MA, USA: Edward Elgar Publishing.

Jennett, N. (1984), 'Attendances, Uncertainty of Outcome and Policy in the Scottish Football League', *Scottish Journal of Political Economy*, 31 (2), 176–98.

Jones, J. (1969), 'The Economics of the National Hockey League', *Canadian Journal of Economics*, 2 (1), 1–20.

Kahane, L. (2006), 'The Reverse-Order-of-Finish Draft in Sports', in W. Andreff and S. Szymanski (eds), *Handbook of Sports Economics*, Cheltenham, UK and Northampton, MA, USA: Edward Elgar Publishing.

Kahn, L.M. (2007), 'Sports League Expansion and Consumer Welfare', *Journal of Sports Economics*, 8 (2), 115–38.

Késenne, S. (1996), 'League Management in Professional Team Sports with Win Maximizing Clubs', *European Journal for Sports Management*, 2 (2), 14–22.

Késenne, S. (2000a), 'Revenue Sharing and Competitive Balance in Professional Team Sports', *Journal of Sports Economics*, 1 (1), 56–65.

Késenne, S. (2000b), 'The Impact of Salary Caps in Professional Team Sports', *Scottish Journal of Political Economy*, 47 (4), 431–55.

Késenne, S. (2003), 'The Salary Cap Proposal of the G-14 in European Football', *European Sports Management Quarterly*, 3 (2), 120–28.

Késenne, S. (2005), 'Revenue Sharing and Competitive Balance: Does the Invariance Proposition Hold?', *Journal of Sports Economics*, 6 (1), 98–106.

Késenne, S. (2006), 'The Win Maximisation Model Reconsidered', *Journal of Sports Economics*, 7 (4), 416–27.

Késenne, S. (2007a), 'Revenue Sharing and Owner Profits', *Journal of Sports Economics*, 8 (5), 519–29.

Késenne, S. (2007b), 'The Peculiar International Economics of Professional Team Sports', *Scottish Journal of Political Economy*, 54 (3), 388–99.

Késenne, S. (2009a), 'The Impact of Pooling and Sharing Broadcast Rights in Professional Team Sports', *International Journal of Sport Finance*, 4 (3), 211–18.

Késenne, S. (2009b), 'The Optimal Size of a Sports League', *International Journal of Sport Finance*, 4 (4), 264–70.

Késenne, S. (2010), 'The Financial Situation of the Football Clubs in the Belgian Jupiler League: Are Players Overpaid in a Win-maximization League?', *International Journal of Sport Finance*, 5 (1), 67–71.

Késenne, S. (2012), 'Can Advertising Make Free-to-Air Broadcasting More Profitable than Pay-TV?', *International Journal of Sport Finance*, 7, 358–64.

Késenne, S. and W. Pauwels (2006), 'Club Objectives and Ticket Pricing in Professional Team Sports', *Eastern Economic Journal*, 32 (3), 549–60.

Koning, R. (2003), 'An Econometric Evaluation of the Effect of Firing a Coach on Team Performance', *Journal of Applied Economics*, 35 (5), 555–64.

Krautmann, A. and L. Hadley (2004), 'Of Dynasties and Dogs', Paper presented at the Sixth International Conference of the International Association of Sports Economists, Athens, Greece, 31 May–2 June.

Kringstad, M. and B. Gerrard (2007), 'Beyond Competitive Balance', in M. Parent and T. Slack (eds), *International Perspectives on the Management of Sport*, Burlington, MA: Elsevier, pp. 149–72.

Lavoie, M. (2000), 'La Proposition d'Invariance dans un Monde où les Equipes Maximisent la Performance Sportive', *Réflets et Perspectives de la Vie Economique*, 39 (2–3), 85–94.

Leeds, M. and P. von Allmen (2011), *The Economics of Sports*, 4th edn, Boston, MA: Addison-Wesley.

Longley, N. (1995), ' Salary Discrimination in the National Hockey League: The Effects of Team Location', *Canadian Public Policy*, 21 (4), 413–22.

Madden, P. (2012), 'Fan Welfare Maximization as a Club Objective in a Professional Sport League', *European Economic Review*, 56 (3), 560–78.

Manasis, Vasileios (2012), 'Quantification of Competitive Balance in Professional Team Sports: Implementation and Empirical Investigation in European Football', Doctoral dissertation, University of Peloponnese, Sparta, Greece.

Marburger, D. (1997a), 'Gate Revenue Sharing and Luxury Taxes in Professional Sports', *Contemporary Economic Policy*, 15 (April), 114–23.

Marburger, D. (ed.) (1997b), *Stee-Rike Four! What's Wrong with the Business of Baseball?*, Westport, CT: Praeger.

Markham, J. and P. Teplitz (1981), *Baseball Economics and Public Policy*, Lexington, MA: Lexington Books, D.C. Heath.

Neale, W. (1964), 'The Peculiar Economics of Professional Sports', *Quarterly Journal of Economics*, 78 (1), 1–14.

Noll, R. (1974a), 'Alternatives in Sports Policy', in R. Noll (ed.), *Government and the Sports Business*, Washington, DC: Brookings Institution, pp. 411–28.

Noll, R. (1974b), 'Attendance and Price Setting', in R. Noll (ed.), *Government and the Sports Business*, Washington, DC: Brookings Institution, pp. 115–58.

Noll, R. (ed.) (1974c), *Government and the Sports Business*, Washington, DC: Brookings Institution.

Noll, R. (1999), 'Competition Policy in European Sports after the Bosman Case', in C. Jeanrenaud and S. Késenne (eds), *Competition Policy in Professional Sports*, Antwerp: Standaard Editions.

Noll, R. (2002), 'The Economics of Promotion and Relegation in Sports Leagues: The Case of English Football', *Journal of Sports Economics*, 3 (2), 169–203.

Noll, R. (2003), 'The Economics of Baseball Contraction', *Journal of Sports Economics*, 4 (4), 367–88.

Peeters, T. (2011), 'Broadcast Rights and Competitive Balance in European Soccer', *International Journal of Sport Finance*, 6 (1), 33–9.

Peeters, T. (2012), 'Media Revenue Sharing as a Coordination Device in Sports Leagues', *International Journal of Industrial Organisation*, 30, 153–63.

Provost, P. (2003), 'Peculiarity of Professional Sports Teams in Europe: The International Transfers', Discussion paper, Université Libre de Bruxelles.

Quirk, J. and M. El-Hodiri (1974), 'The Economic Theory of a Professional League', in R. Noll (ed.), *Government and the Sports Business*, Washington, DC: Brookings Institution, pp. 33–80.

Quirk, J. and R. Fort (1992), *Pay Dirt: The Business of Professional Team Sports*, Princeton, NJ: Princeton University Press.

Quirk, J. and R. Fort (1999), *Hard Ball: The Abuse of Power in Pro Team Sports*, Princeton, NJ: Princeton University Press.

Rascher, D. (1997), 'A Model of a Professional Sports League', in W. Hendricks (ed.), *Advances in the Economics of Sport*, Vol. 2, Greenwich, CT and London: JAI Press, pp. 27–76.

Rosen, S. (1981), 'The Economics of Superstars', *American Economic Review*, 71 (4), 845–98.

Ross, S. (1991), 'Break Up the Sports League Monopolies', in P. Staudohar and J. Mangan (eds), *The Business of Professional Sports*, Urbana: University of Illinois Press.

Rottenberg, S. (1956), 'The Baseball Players' Labor Market', *Journal of Political Economy*, 64 (3), 242–58.

Sanderson, A. (2002), 'The Many Dimensions of Competitive Balance', *Journal of Sports Economics*, 3 (2), 204–28.

Sandy, R., P. Sloane and M. Rosentraub (2004), *The Economics of Sport: An International Perspective*, New York: Palgrave Macmillan.

Scully, G. (1974), 'Pay and Performance in Major League Baseball', *American Economic Review*, 64 (6), 915–30.

Scully, G. (1989), *The Business of Major League Baseball*, Chicago: University of Chicago Press.

Scully, G. (ed.) (1992), *Advances in the Economics of Sport*, Vol.1, Greenwich, CT: JAI Press.

Scully, G. (1995), *The Market Structure of Sports*, Chicago, IL: University of Chicago Press.

Scully, G. (1999), 'Free Agency and the Rate of Monopsonistic Exploitation in Baseball', in C. Jeanrenaud and S. Késenne (eds), *Competition Policy in Professional Sports*, Antwerp: Standaard Editions.

Siegfried, J. and C. Hinshaw (1979), 'The Effects of Lifting TV Blackouts on Professional Football No-Shows', *Journal of Economics and Business*, 32 (1), 1–13.

Simmons, R. (2006), 'Demand for Spectator Sports', in S. Szymanski and W. Andreff (eds), *Handbook of the Economics of Sport*, Cheltenham, UK and Northampton, MA, USA: Edward Elgar Publishing, pp. 77–89.

Simmons, R. and B. Buraimo (2005), 'Television Viewing and Stadium Attendance: Cannibalization or Complements?', Working paper, Lancaster University, UK.

Sloane, P. (1969), 'The Labour Market in Professional Football', *British Journal of Industrial Relations*, 7 (2), 181–99.

Sloane, P. (1971), 'The Economics of Professional Football: The Football Club as a Utility Maximiser', *Scottish Journal of Political Economy*, 17 (2), 121–46.

Sloane, P. (1980), *Sport in the Market?*, Hobart Paper No. 85, London: Institute of Economic Affairs.

Solow, R. (1979), 'Another Possible Source of Wage Stickiness', *Journal of Macroeconomics*, 1 (1), 79–82.

Sommers, P. (1992), *Diamonds Are Forever: The Business of Baseball*, Washington, DC: Brookings Institution.

Staudohar, P. (1999), 'Labor Relations in Basketball: The Lockout of 1998–99', *Monthly Labor Review* (US Department of Labor), April, 3–9.

Staudohar, P. and J. Mangan (eds) (1991), *The Business of Professional Sports*, Urbana and Chicago: University of Illinois Press.

Szymanski, S. (2001), 'Income Inequality, Competitive Balance and Attractiveness of Team Sports: Some Evidence and a Natural Experiment from English Soccer', *Economic Journal*, III (469), F4–F26.

Szymanski, S. (2003), 'The Economic Design of Sporting Contests', *Journal of Economic Literature*, 41 (4), 1137–87.

Szymanski, S. (2004), 'Professional Team Sports Are a Game: The Walrasian Fixed-Supply Conjecture Model, Contest-Nash Equilibrium, and the Invariance Principle', *Journal of Sports Economics*, 5 (2), 111–26.

Szymanski, S. (2006), 'The Theory of Contests', in J. Fizel (ed.), *Handbook of Sports Economics Research*, London: M.E. Sharpe.

Szymanski, S. and S. Késenne (2004), 'Competitive Balance and Gate Revenue Sharing in Team Sports', *Journal of Industrial Economics*, 51 (4), 513–25.

Szymanski, S. and T. Kuypers (1999), *Winners and Losers: The Business Strategy of Football*, London: Viking.

Szymanski, S. and S. Leach (2005), 'Tilting the Playing Field: Why a Sports League Planner Would Choose Less, Not More, Competitive Balance', Working paper, Tanaka Business School, Imperial College, London.

Vrooman, J. (1995), 'A General Theory of Professional Sports Leagues', *Southern Economic Journal*, 61 (4), 971–90.

Vrooman, J. (1996), 'The Baseball Player's Labor Market Reconsidered', *Southern Economic Journal*, 63 (2), 339–60.

Vrooman, J. (1997), 'Franchise Free Agency in Professional Sports Leagues', *Southern Economic Journal*, 64 (1), 191–219.

Vrooman, J. (2000), 'The Economics of American Sports Leagues', *Scottish Journal of Political Economy*, 47 (4), 364–98.

Vrooman, J. (2007), 'Theory of the Beautiful Game: The Unification of European Football', *Scottish Journal of Political Economy*, 54 (3), 314–54.

Weitzman, M. (1984), *The Share Economy: Conquering Stagflation*, Cambridge, MA: Harvard University Press.

Wiseman, N. (1977), 'The Economics of Football', *Lloyds Bank Review*, 123, 29–43.

Zimbalist, A. (1992), *Baseball and Billions*, New York: Basic Books.

Zimbalist, A. (ed.) (2001), *The Economics of Sport*, Vols 1 and 2, Cheltenham, UK and Northampton, MA, USA: Edward Elgar Publishing.

Zimbalist, A. (2003), 'Sport as Business', *Oxford Review of Economic Policy*, 19 (4), 503–11.

Index